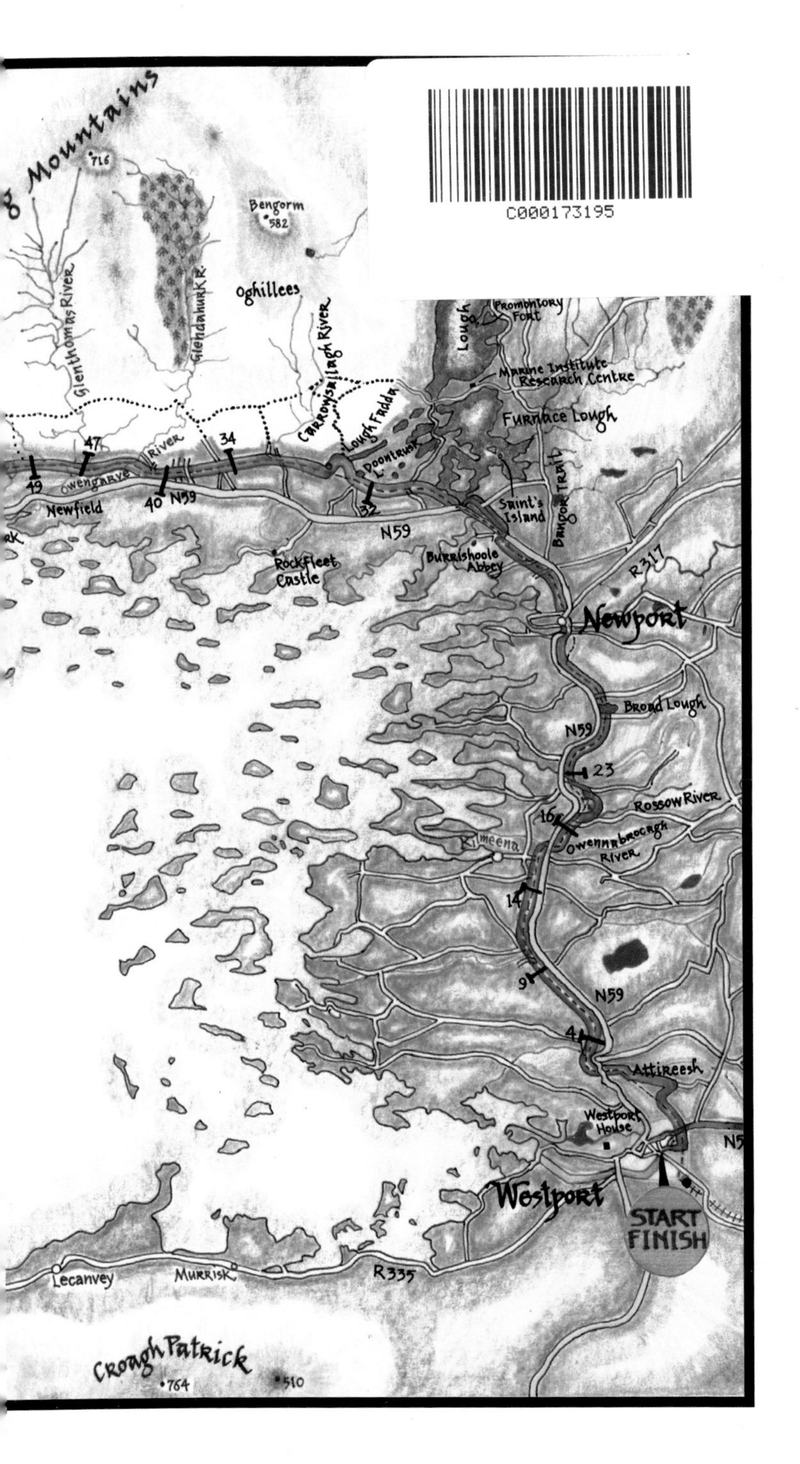

Mountains
716
Bengorm
582
Glenthomas River
Glendahurk R.
Oghillees
Carrowsallagh River
Lough
Promontory Fort
Marine Institute Research Centre
Furnace Lough
Lough Fadda
Doontrusk L.
47
34
49
40
32
River
Owengarve
N59
Newfield
Saint's Island
Bangor Trail
Rockfleet Castle
Burrishoole Abbey
R317
Newport
Broad Lough
23
Rossow River
16
Owennabrocagh River
Kilmeena
14
9
4
Attireesh
Westport House
Westport
START
FINISH
Lecanvey
Murrisk
R335
Croagh Patrick
764
510

THE GREAT WESTERN GREENWAY

A Guide to Walking and Cycling
from Westport to Achill

The Wildlife, Flora, and History
Along the Way

Iris Galloway

This publication has received support from
the Heritage Council under the 2012 Heritage Education,
Community and Outreach Grant Scheme.

Published by
PROSPECT PUBLISHING
Prospect, Westport, County Mayo, Ireland

Designed by Fergus Kelly ••• ellipsis.ie
Printed in Ireland by Walsh Colour Print
Bound by Kavanagh Bookbinding

ISBN 978-0-9574303-0-3

Contents

Introduction

"The best way to see a country is from the footplate of a locomotive." George Dow

The Great Western Greenway wraps around the eastern and northern rims of Clew Bay on the west coast of Co. Mayo, Ireland. This broad, sparkling bay is overlooked by the distinctive pyramid-shaped peak of Croagh Patrick on the south shore and by Corraun Hill and the picturesque Nephin Beg mountain range to the north. Humpbacked Clare Island looms like a fortress against the sweeping Atlantic swell to the west.

This is the breathtaking backdrop to the longest off-road cycle and walking trail in Ireland. Built upon the old railway line between Achill Sound in the north and Westport to the southeast of the bay, it extends for 43.5km (27 miles).

It is exciting to think that in these days, when the automobile is king of domestic travel, we can still transport ourselves along this historic railway track. Although the tracks themselves were removed long ago, the rail corridor has now been cleared of its tangled undergrowth, allowing us to cover the distance on foot or bicycle, safely segregated from motor traffic.

As the gradient of a railway must be relatively level in order for a locomotive to pull its heavy load, the majority of the Greenway is accessible to all the family. Most of it is ideally suited for walkers and cyclists, strollers and wheelchairs.

Railways have always been a valuable means of forging connections between distant communities, and it is fascinating to retrace the steps our forebears took to open up the West.

In a time when travel upon utterly decrepit roads was accomplished by horse and carriage or donkey and cart or simply on foot, what a profound difference the advent of the railway must have made to a remote enclave such as Achill

Achill Village Scene (Lawrence Collection, courtesy of the National Library of Ireland)

Island. For many years it was a lifeline for the Achill Islanders, many of whom left the island seasonally for England and Scotland to work in the potato fields.

The railway made both Achill and Mulranny more accessible to tourists and stimulated commerce. It vitalised business in Newport and Westport, linking up with the busy shipping port down at Westport Quay.

However, times change, and improved roads as well as the increasing popularity of the motor car spelled an end to the era of the train. Although Westport is still connected to Dublin by rail, all the lines between Westport Quay and Achill closed down one by one, only a few decades after they were built.

Whilst the last train to Achill plied its way in 1937, and the line was left to nature for a couple of generations, there are still remnants of the old days of rail travel along the way. The original train stations still exist; some remain in use in other capacities, while one and parts of others have fallen into ruins.

Some of the old railway cottages, where those who operated the level crossings dwelled, are still occupied. The beautiful stone railway bridges and viaducts have survived, though many are not in use.

The old Midland Great Western Railway Hotel, now called Mulranny Park Hotel, fell into neglect for many years and is now restored and open to the public.

Thanks to the vision of those involved in the intricate task of reclaiming the rail corridor between Westport and Newport, and to the 161 landowners that gave their permission for the route to run through their lands, anyone can now travel along the gentle gradient of the old railway line through the spectacular scenery of Ireland's west coast.

Hiking or biking, one passes through a pristine backdrop of soaring mountains, glittering sea, foaming rivers, shimmering lakes, open bogland and rolling pastures, surrounded by wildflowers and birdsong.

The Greenway is a living, ever-changing entity, and a book such as this can never be complete. But my hope is that in some small measure it may enhance your experience of the journey by supplying a taste of history and a bit of information about the rich biodiversity of the territory and by pointing out other features of interest along the way.

As E. M. Forster said,

"Railway termini are our gates to the glorious and the unknown. Through them we pass out into adventure and sunshine...."

Westport to Quay tracks through bridge with Reek in background (Lawrence Collection, courtesy of the National Library of Ireland)

Railway History

On the 9th of October 1834 Ireland's first railway opened, spanning the distance between Dublin and Kingstown Harbour (Dún Laoghaire), 10km (6 miles) to the south. Eight carriages were pulled by the steam locomotive 'Hibernia'.

From this starting point, the history of the many different railways that operated in early times is fairly complex, with independent railway companies competing for territory, forging agreements and amalgamating.

There were separate lines in Northern Ireland, Cork, Dublin and Donegal. Between 1834 and 1846 there were four main lines originating out of Dublin, and for many years these were unconnected with one another.

The line from Dublin did not reach Co. Mayo until 1861, when the track from Castlerea, Co. Roscommon to Ballyhaunis was opened by the Midland & Great Western Railway. The MGWR, established in the 1840s, was the third largest company in Ireland.

The following year, in May, the line was extended to Claremorris and from there to Castlebar in December. Further progress was delayed by financial pressures, and it was not until four years later, on the 24th of January 1866, that

Above: Castlebar Railway Station (Lawrence Collection, courtesy of the National Library of Ireland). Left: Westport Railway Station by permission of Westport Railway Station.

Achill Railway Station (Lawrence Collection, courtesy of the National Library of Ireland)

the line to Westport was opened. In 1874 an extension to the bustling Quay at Westport Harbour was added.

Balfour Lines

Several years after this, new legislation was introduced with the purpose of providing funding for narrow-gauge rail transport to disadvantaged regions of the country. The Act was put forward by Arthur J. Balfour, who was Chief Secretary of Ireland between 1887 and 1891. A line was proposed from Westport to Achill, thereafter known as one of the 'Balfour Lines'.

The first stage of this was completed on the 1st of February 1884, when the line to Newport was opened. Later that year, on the 1st of August, the track to Mulranny was inaugurated. The following year, on the 13th of May 1895, the line to Achill was completed.

This section terminated at Achill Sound, just across from Achill Island, Ireland's largest island, and home to almost 4,700 people. A swing bridge, opened in 1888, connected the island to the mainland by road across the narrow, but fierce channel.

However, the roads at that time were appalling, rendering travel by road quite an ordeal. Therefore, the line to Achill met with great success; it made the island more accessible, encouraging tourism and trade. It also improved the postal system and created jobs in the construction and maintenance of the railway.

Fair-days once a month brought crowds of cattle-traders, and the trains carried fish and eggs up to Dublin daily. Later, in the 1930s, a government incentive was put in place to encourage people in poorer areas of the west to harvest more turf and send it to Dublin by train. Under this scheme a considerable amount of turf was taken from Achill up to Dublin.

Achill Island

Achill is about 86% peat bog, and in the 19th century about 14% of the land was farmed. Of this, about 15% was devoted to the growth of corn (grain), 9% was used for grazing cattle and sheep, and the remainder was comprised of hayfields and vegetable plots.

People supplemented their diet by fishing in the rivers, lakes and sea, but in general there was little work available, and many islanders travelled to Scotland and England to work in the fields picking potatoes. These people were known as 'tattie hokers'.

The conditions in the potato fields were harsh and the wages were poor, but during the season the tattie hokers were able to make enough money to be able to survive at home for the rest of the year. The following is a ditty that used to be sung in the fields:

So now I'm a worker in a tatty hoking squad
And when we see the merchant coming
We all start going mad.
It's helter skelter up the drills,
Each one to beat his mate,
To sit outside and watch the fun,
It is really great!
We're up and out each morning
Before the dawning of the day,
With the gaffer cracking matches

Hooker by swing bridge on Achill Sound (Lawrence Collection, courtesy of the National Library of Ireland)

Out before us on the way.
But I'd rather be in Achill
With 'pardógs' on the ass
And walk to Dookinella
Three miles to holy Mass.

(The above ditty was taken from Safe-Home Programme Ireland. A pardóg is a pair of creels which is strapped to a donkey's back for transporting turf. Dookinella is a small village in Achill.)

Before the arrival of the train, the tattie hokers had to cross Clew Bay to Westport on native sailing boats called hookers, and from there transfer onto a steam packet which brought them to England or Scotland.

The advent of the train to Achill Sound made the journey much easier for the hundreds of migrant workers heading off to the potato fields. They travelled up to Dublin on special trains called 'harvesters', and from there caught a ship across the Irish Sea.

However, this development was overshadowed by a prediction made two centuries earlier by Brian Rua Ó Ceabháin from Erris, who was granted powers of prophesy when he was extraordinarily kind to a widow. He foresaw that "carriages on iron wheels, emitting smoke and fire, would carry coffins on both their first and last journeys."

In 1895, a week before the railway line to Achill was completed, four hookers left Achill full of tattie hokers bound for Westport to meet the Glasgow packet. As they neared the Quay, the ship came into view, standing out on the tide. Most of those on board one of the hookers, called the *Victory*, rushed to one side of the boat to get a better view of the ship, causing the hooker to list.

It was a fairly calm day, but a sudden gust of wind came up, seizing the sail and flinging the boom to the same side of the boat, which capsized as a result. All on deck were thrown into the sea, and many were trapped under the heavy sail and drowned. All but one person below decks were drowned when water flooded into the hold.

The other hookers and the crew of the Glasgow ship rushed to help, but nevertheless, 34 people lost their lives. This tragedy came to be known as the Clew Bay Disaster.

The bodies were gathered up and laid out upon the Quay, where they were placed into coffins. Although the railway to Achill was not yet in operation, a special train was commissioned to bring the dead back to Achill. Hundreds of people gathered at points along the way to pay their respects to the dead. Thus was the first part of Brian Rua's prophecy fulfilled.

Mulranny

While Achill continued to prosper from the arrival of the railway, other towns along the route did as well. Mulranny, or Malaranny as it was always referred to by the railway, is situated between Newport and Achill. Maoil Raithne or Malla Raithne means 'Hill of the Ferns'. At that time it was just a small settlement, but its scenic beauty came to the attention of officials, and to encourage tourism, the MGWR opened a hotel there in 1897.

The hotel was built on a rise above the town, with spectacular views across Clew Bay to Croagh Patrick and foaming surf breaking on magnificent white sandy beaches below.

Achill Islanders circa 1880 - 1890 (Lawrence Collection, courtesy of the National Library of Ireland)

The luxury hotel had all the modern conveniences of the time, including electric lights. By 1900 it was also equipped with hot- and cold-water baths, and guests had access to the hotel's private golf links and boats.

A causeway was built by the company across the shallow Trawoughter Bay in front of the hotel to give visitors access to the beach out at the end. This still exists, and provides a delightful walk across the bay.

In later years a large outdoor seawater swimming pool was added, with salt water pumped up from the sea below. The pumphouse is still visible today beside the steps down to the beach, though the pool itself has been replaced in recent times by a modern indoor fresh-water facility.

The year after the hotel was built, the MGWR offered a combined rail and hotel ticket, one of the first of its kind. It proved to be a popular attraction and was still on offer in 1922, when it cost £2.30 for a return ticket from Westport to Mulranny, including an overnight stay with dinner.

That same year, the political unrest in the country reached the hotel, when it was occupied by the Irregulars. During their

TOP: Mulranny Railway Station (Lawrence Collection, courtesy of the National Library of Ireland)
LEFT: MGWR Hotel, later the Great Southern, with Causeway (Lawrence Collection, courtesy of the National Library of Ireland)
RIGHT: The Great Southern Hotel, now called Mulranny Park Hotel

residency they contrived to construct a couple of armoured cars out of boilers taken from the hotel.

Among these was the most famous of such vehicles built at the time, dubbed the 'Queen of the West'. In 1922 she took part in a battle near Clifden in Co. Galway, and was captured by the National Army. She was renamed 'The Girl I Left Behind Me' and was used for a short while before being abandoned in a bog.

The following year the hotel was taken over by the National Army. During these occupations much damage was caused to the hotel, which took an entire year to rectify.

In 1925 the MGWR merged with the Great Southern Railway, which renamed the hotel the Great Southern Hotel. This was one of several hotels owned by the railway. After the railway closed down, the GSR retained the hotel and arranged for a bus service to bring in tourists.

In 1945 the GSR was absorbed by CIÉ, and around this time tourists began to travel abroad for holidays. Business continued to falter, and in 1991 the hotel shut its doors for the last time. It became derelict, but in 2003 was purchased by new owners who restored the hotel and re-opened its doors in 2005.

Newport

Newport, formerly called Ballyveaghan (from Baile Uí Fhiacháin, meaning 'Feehan's Town'), was founded in the 18th century by the Medlycot landowners, through their land agent, Captain Pratt. Its site was chosen

Newport Railway Station with tunnel across viaduct (Lawrence Collection, courtesy of the National Library of Ireland)

Viaduct in Newport

largely because the tidal river could accommodate merchant ships of up to 500 tonnes.

Captain Pratt introduced linen production to the town and brought a community of Quakers from Ulster to manage the business, owing to their reputation for honesty and diligence.

Under their management the industry prospered, but after some years the Quakers ran into a fundamental problem. They only married within their own faith, and the nearest Quaker colony was in Roscommon. They soon began to run out of possibilities within their own community in Newport, as they were all closely related to each other.

In 1739 they decided to move to Roscommon to be near the other Quaker settlement. Nevertheless the linen industry continued to thrive until the early 19th century, when the bulk of commerce shifted to Westport.

In the late 1700s the Medlycot Estate was taken over by the O'Donels, who built Newport House, overlooking the quay. The town once again began to prosper, and in the early 1800s the population expanded to over 12,000 people. This, however, was decimated during the ensuing Great Famine in the 1840s, due to disease, starvation and mass emigration.

After the Famine a merchant named Martin Carey began to rebuild trade and industry in the town. Towards the end of the century the Carey family were responsible for the erection of many of the buildings that are still there today. In 1894 a school for lace-making was established, which flourished until the lace industry collapsed after WWII.

In the last decade of the 1800s the railway came to Newport. A graceful 92m (305ft) viaduct was built across the Black Oak River, which runs through the centre of town. It was constructed of local red sandstone with limestone facings and featured seven arches. It cost £7,640 to complete.

A tunnel was built near its south end in 1892, with another further south, and in February 1894 the first train chugged its way across the viaduct.

The End of the Railway

While the railway was of great social and economic benefit to the whole area, it did not reach the levels of usage originally expected, and the improvement of road systems in the 1930s, along with the growing popularity of cars, brought an end to the Westport-Achill line soon thereafter.

In 1934, much to the dismay of the Achill people, the passenger service was terminated. Only freight trains continued to run, except for a short period in 1936 when passenger trains were reinstated because the condition of the roads was unsuitable for the replacement bus. The passenger train was discontinued for good after the road was repaired, and the freight service ceased in September 1937.

All railway fixtures had been removed except the rails themselves, when disastrous news arrived of the death of ten young Achill men who had been working in the potato fields in Kirkintilloch, near Glasgow. All ten had been trapped inside a bothy, or cabin, which caught on fire in the night, and were burnt to death.

Their bodies were shipped to Dublin, from where they were brought by a specially commissioned train back to Achill, the last one ever to run on that line. Word of the disaster spread across the country, and huge crowds turned out along the way to offer their sympathy to the relatives of the victims.

The ten coffins were buried in a special plot in Kildownet Cemetery on Achill Island. Thus was the second part of Brian Rua's sinister prophesy fulfilled.

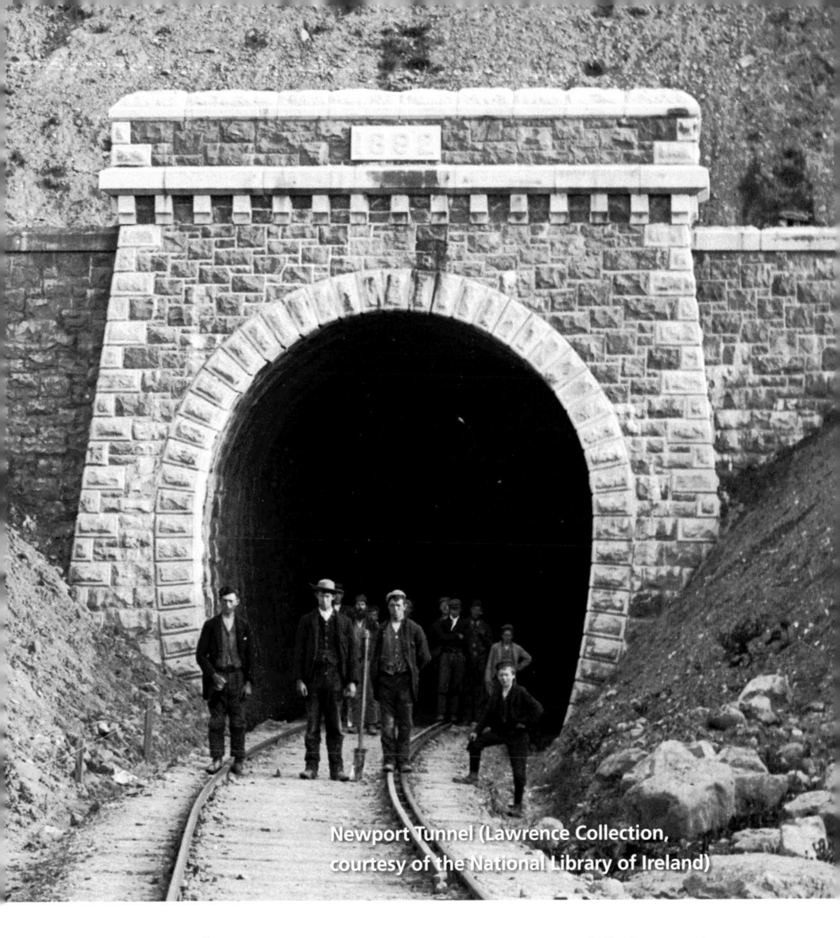

Newport Tunnel (Lawrence Collection, courtesy of the National Library of Ireland)

In 1938 CIÉ, the Irish Transport System, began to lift the steel tracks. This was during the lead-up to World War II, and they were all sold to Germany, which was hungry for steel.

The passenger train from Westport to the Quay had also shut down, though much earlier, in 1901. After that, a freight train still operated up until the early 1980s. The train from Dublin to Westport still runs, with up to four trains a day.

Today the Achill to Westport trains are but an echo of the past, but thanks to the vision of those involved in the development of the Greenway, pedestrians and cyclists can now retrace the scenic route of the old locomotives.

Overview of the Greenway

The Great Western Greenway runs along the eastern and northern coasts of Clew Bay. Cuan Mó is the Irish name for this stretch of water, meaning "large bay." A broad, relatively shallow bay, it measures roughly 13km (8 miles) across, from north to south, and 27km (16.8 miles) from the eastern shore to Clare Island in the west.

Westport lies at the southeastern corner, and Newport 12.5km (7.8 miles) away at the northeastern corner. Mulranny is 18km (11 miles) to the west of Newport, with Achill Sound another 13km (8 miles) along to the northwest.

The entire Greenway is 43.5km (27 miles) from start to finish, and while some individuals may want to tackle it all in one go, others will want to do it in segments. Therefore, this part of the book is divided into three sections: Westport to Newport, Newport to Mulranny and Mulranny to Achill. These are the sites of the old railway stations and are good places to start and finish, having plentiful parking and places to find refreshment.

Bring along rain-gear, liquid, snacks, a mobile phone and, if you are biking, a helmet and high-visibility clothing.

If you are cycling and you see a pedestrian ahead, **please ring your bell** or call out politely. Walkers are very often unaware of your approach and highly appreciate being warned, as this avoids accidents and sudden alarm. Cyclists should always give way to pedestrians.

The Greenway trail is clearly waymarked at many points, using the National Cycle Network symbol and white directional arrows.

Near main access points and information boards you will find QR codes which a smartphone will read. These provide a link to the Greenway website, greenway.ie, as well as the Greenway iPhone app.

In the book I have assigned numbers to all the gates, starting from Westport, as points of reference. The gates themselves are not actually numbered along the Greenway, but some are marked on the maps in this book.

In the following three sections, a description of the layout of the Greenway itself forms the main body of the text. Additional points of interest are supplied in coloured boxes, the key to which is as follows:

Environment

History

General

In an emergency, ring 999 for emergency services.

Please remember to:

- Leave only tracks and take only photographs.
- Dispose of waste properly.
- Leave cultural, historic or natural objects undisturbed.
- Respect wildlife and farmstock.
- Always make sure to re-shut closed farm gates.
- Show consideration to other Greenway users.
- Be careful not to start fires.
- Plan ahead and prepare for your excursion.

I have arbitrarily chosen to orientate the book starting from Westport and ending at Achill, so if you are traveling the Greenway in the opposite direction, I'm afraid you will have to turn the book upside-down.

Furnace Lough
34
Doontrusk L.
32
Saint's Island
Bangor Trail
N59
Rockfleet Castle
Burrishoole Abbey
R317
Newport
Broad Lough
N59
23
Rossow River
16
Owennabrocagh River
Kilmeena
14
9
N59
4
Attireesh
Westport House
Westport
START
FINISH
R335

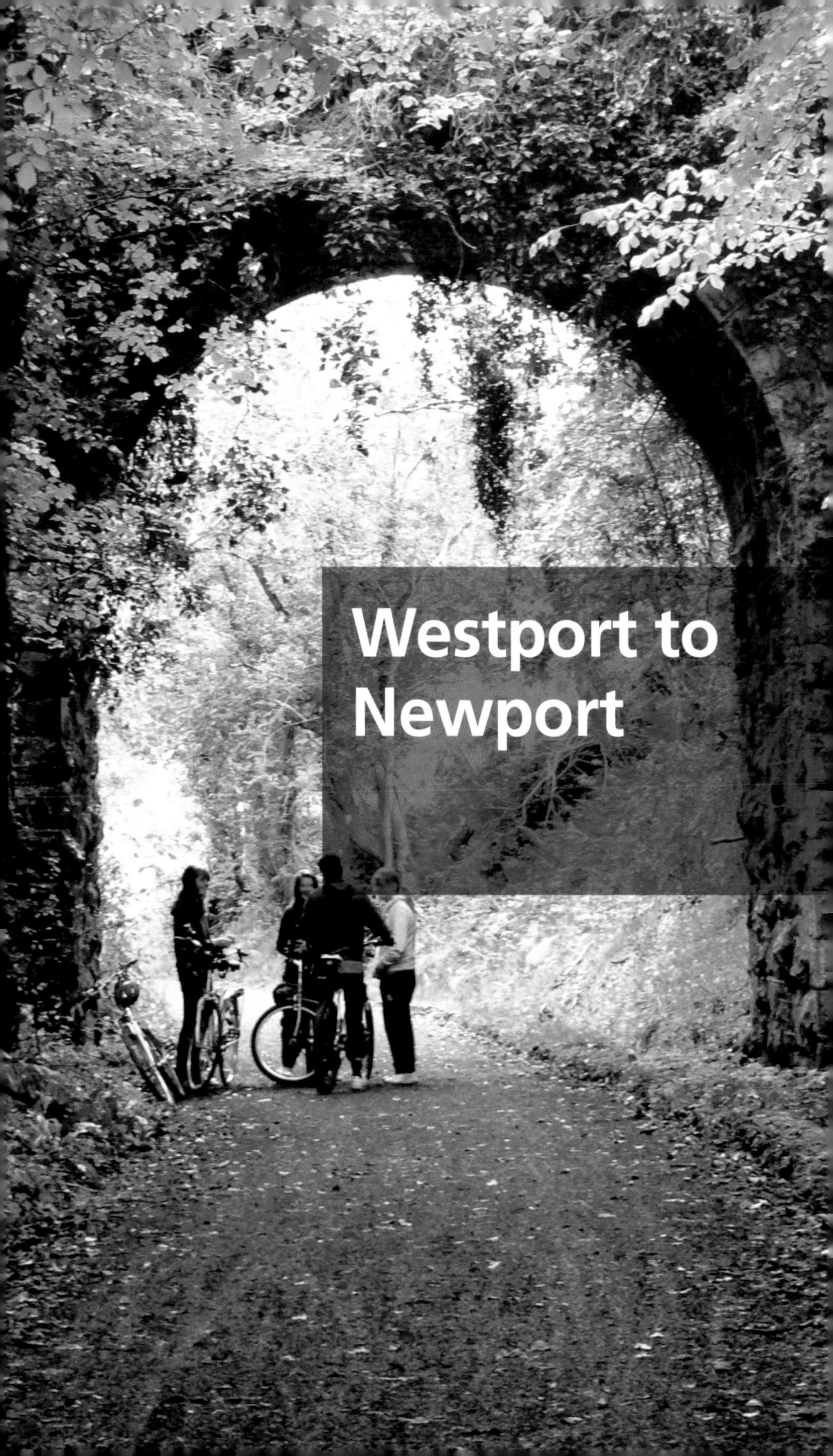
Westport to
Newport

In a Nutshell

The distance from **Westport to Newport** is 12.5km (7.8 miles). The estimated cycling time is 1–1½ hours, while walking should take 3–3½ hours.

The beginning of the Westport to Newport section takes you well off the main road and around behind an old convent to connect up with the original track, which crosses a beautiful old stone viaduct.

It then skirts the sports field of a school, crosses a main road, and runs for a short distance along a side road, before leaving traffic behind altogether. It runs beneath several fine old arched bridges, and through overhanging trees.

After about 2km it runs parallel to the main road through open fields and thin woodland. At times it runs directly next to the road, whilst in other places there is a bank or hedgerow in between.

After about 3km farther it veers off across wet grasslands, crossing a couple of bridges, before once again following close beside the road. After about 2km more, you coast into the charming town of Newport.

Westport's Setting

Croagh Patrick

Westport has always been associated with Croagh Patrick, which crowns the south side of the Bay about 8km (5 miles) southwest of Westport town. This peak is known locally as the Reek and is Ireland's holiest mountain. At 764m (2,507ft), it is the third highest mountain in Mayo.

It has been a sacred site since pre-Christian times, when it was called Cruachán Aigle, nowadays said to mean 'Eagle Mountain'. There is some evidence that it was the site of a Bronze-Age hillfort (circa 1,000 B.C.) and that its distinctive conical shape would have been regarded as being of great spiritual significance by the people of that time, perhaps by Druidic practitioners.

Croagh Patrick

The existing chapel at the top was built in 1905, but there are much older remains of Early Christian structures nearby, some dating to the 9th century. In the 5th century St. Patrick is said to have fasted on the peak for 40 days and 40 nights and to have banished all the snakes from Ireland when his fast was over.

The mountain is a pilgrimage site, and many thousands of people climb to the chapel on the top every year, especially on Reek Sunday, the last Sunday of July, when multitudes of the devout flock together to complete the arduous climb. This date falls very close to the ancient Celtic festival of Lughnasa, which celebrated Lugh, the god of light, and the beginning of harvest.

An ancient Christian pilgrimage trail, called the Tóchar Phádraic ('Patrick's Causeway'), runs from Ballintubber Abbey in the east to the top of the Reek, a distance of 35.4km (22 miles). This follows a pre-Christian trail that probably originated around 350 AD and ran from Ráth Cruachán in Co. Roscommon to Cruachán Aigle. Ráth Cruachán is believed to have been the royal seat of Connacht.

St. Dabeoc's Heath

Since St. Patrick's time Christian pilgrims have come from far and wide to follow this walk. It is said that sojourners from Portugal wore a sprig of St. Dabeoc's Heather pinned to their traveling cloaks, which spread its seeds along the route, and that this is why this striking large-belled heather is found only in the west of Ireland today.

Traditionally pilgrims often concluded their journey at tiny Caher Island, just south of Clare Island. Nowadays it is uninhabited, but there are remains of an Early Christian monastery on the island, thought to date back to the 7th century. A stone enclosure contains a ruined chapel, and there are several carved stone crosses. The island's name in Irish, Cathair na Naomh, means 'circular stone fort of the saints'.

Clew Bay

The inner reaches of Clew Bay consist of an extraordinary landscape of drowned drumlins - small, elongated humps composed of glacial sediments left behind by the retreating glaciers at the end of the last ice age and inundated by the rising sea levels resulting from the melting ice.

Clew Bay viewed from the top of Croagh Patrick

It is said that there are 365 islands, one for every day of the year. In the mid-1880s 12 of the islands were inhabited, with over 800 islanders all told. Today the permanent population numbers only about 20.

Westport Town

The drumlins extend inland, and Westport town is built in their midst. There are two centres to Westport; one is the main town, which is built along the Carrowbeg River flowing through the middle of the town, and the other is the Quay area, which sprang up around the tidal inlet at the mouth of the river.

This area is rich in marine and bird life, and even Otters and Seals can be seen along the Quay. The undulating land between Westport and Newport is testament to the presence of drumlins deposited by the last great glaciation about 10,000 years ago. These are underlain, for the most part, by carboniferous limestone.

Westport in Irish is Cathair na Mart, meaning 'circular stone fort of the beeves'. It is one of Ireland's few planned towns. Originally the village was positioned down by the estuary near Westport House, which itself was built in the 1730s on the site of an old O'Malley castle. The castle's dungeon is still part of the house.

The O'Malleys were the chief seafaring clan in the region, and Grace O'Malley, otherwise known as Granuaile the pirate queen, was a powerful leading figure in the 16th century. The Brownes of Westport House are her direct descendants.

In 1780 John Browne, the Earl of Altamont, decided to move the village farther inland. He commissioned a renowned Georgian architect named James Wyatt to design the town around the Carrowbeg River, an area which is now called the Mall. The earl was also responsible for instigating the linen industry in the town.

Westport town and port became a busy centre of trade, with linen and cotton mills, breweries, an extensive whiskey distillery, a herring fishery, corn and flour mills, a clog factory and a tannery.

Today, Westport is still a thriving town of about 5,500 people. There is a great variety of businesses in the town, and many artists, craftspeople and writers live in the area, which is predominantly surrounded by farmland.

Traditional music can be found in the pubs every night of the week, and there are numerous festivals throughout the year. There is a food and craft market every Saturday along the Mall, which includes the maker of Carrowholly Cheese, a member of the Gourmet Greenway Trail devised by Mulranny Park Hotel to showcase various artisan food producers in the vicinity of the Greenway. Carrawholly Cheese is a Gouda-style cheese, hand-crafted from local raw cow's milk, using vegetarian rennet. For more information or to ask about tours, you can email: carrowhollycheese@gmail.com.

Also included in the Gourmet Greenway Trail is An Port Mór Restaurant, located on Brewery Lane. Here the use of local, seasonal and artisan produce is highlighted, with an emphasis on fresh seafood. You can check them out at www.anportmor.com.

To have a look at other participants in the Gourmet Greenway Trail, you can view their brochure at www.newporthouse.ie/GourmetGreenway_brochure.pdf.

The Mall

Westport Viaduct (Lawrence Collection, courtesy of National Library of Ireland)

Old Railway Line Walk

Another feature worth exploring is the Old Railway Line Walk from the centre of town down to the Quay. This is an old railway line that was turned into a walking and biking trail several years ago and is also known as the Westport Greenway.

The walk can be accessed from the south side of Altamount Street, across from the old convent on the road towards the Railway Station, along what is referred to as the 'cattle pass'. If you would like more information on this walk, you might like to read *Walk the Line: Pocket Guide to the Old Railway Line, Westport*, produced by Westport Civic Trust.

Out From Westport

Start of the Great Western Greenway

The Great Western Greenway starts across the street from the point where the Westport Greenway comes out onto Altamount Street (which leads to the Railway Station) at the 'cattle pass'.

Go directly across the road near the roundabout on Altamount Street and turn left onto Distillery Road. Straight ahead you will see Clew Bay Bike Hire. To the right of this is Mill Road, which you turn right onto, passing the Westport Social Service Centre on your right, and next, on the same side, you will see a gap in the stone wall with a bollard and blue emblem of walkers and a cyclist.

Follow this pathway up between a hedgerow and a green wire fence, beyond which is the old Sisters of Mercy Convent, founded in 1842 and vacated in 2008. At the top of this section you pass between two stone gateposts. Straight ahead you will see the beginning of an old stone viaduct with seven arches.

Westport Viaduct

Here a path to your left winds down under the last arch to a car park below. To remain on the Greenway, follow straight on and turn left, continuing on over the viaduct. (If you turn right here instead, you go along the original track to a steel bridge which crosses Altamount Street to Westport Railway Station. The bridge, however, is blocked off by a high concrete wall, and you can go no farther along here.)

The viaduct brings you across above a meadow and small river, high up in the tree-tops of Ash, Sycamore, Beech and Holly. Most of these trees have grown up since the Lawrence Collection photograph was made around the turn of the last century.

Sports Field

At the end of the viaduct the path takes a sharp right-hand bend. The original railway track went straight on across what is now the sports field for Rice College. The path now skirts the field and joins up with the original track on the other side.

The grassy verges along here are full of wildflowers, including bright yellow Tormentil, Smooth Hawksbeard, Kidney Vetch and Meadow Vetchling, Red and White Clover, the white trumpets of Bindweed, the electric purple-blue feathery clusters of Tufted Vetch, and the uncommon pink sprig of Centaury.

Tufted Vetch

The path goes close along the edge of a large patch of woodland called Colonel's or Knockranny Woods, interspersed with walking trails. A short way along here the path splits in two, and you go left, continuing on around the sports field. To your right is a high stoney bank which was gouged out of the landscape to make room for the Greenway to go around the sports field. In time, this will be covered with plants.

After this, the pathway veers to the right, proceeding between green wire fences entwined with wildflowers and passing through a grove of trees with a high bank to the right. This section follows the original track, which crossed the viaduct behind you and ran straight across the present sports field to this point.

The N5

The path rises slightly and then dips to pass beneath an old stone archway. On the other side of this you come to the main Westport-Castlebar road, or the N5, which is extremely busy. There are plans to put traffic-calming measures in place here, but be very vigilant crossing this road.

The path continues along the small road on the other side, up past a housing estate to the left and the Allergan factory to the right. Once you are past this section you will

Wall Brown Butterflies

On a sunny day you may see Wall Brown butterflies resting on the warm stones, though they are very alert and easily startled. They may be hard to spot, as their markings blend in with the mottled designs on the stones.

Brown butterflies, of the family Satyridae, often have 'eye spots' on their wings, which are believed to protect them from predators. This may be because they imitate eyes and thus appear intimidating to would-be attackers, or possibly because the spots are conspicuous, and predators aim for the spots rather than the body of the butterfly, resulting only in slight wing damage. They may also be a signal between mating butterflies.

come to a roundabout. Immediately to the left of this you will see two stone gateposts, and the Greenway resumes just to the left of these.

Off-Road Past Allergan

Directly to the left of the Greenway entry is a driveway down to a private house called 'The Deerpark'. The original railway track went along this driveway and came out at Attireesh, which you will reach shortly.

The path crosses over a ditch and continues along to the right of it, then takes a 90-degree turn to the right and runs between grassy fields for a short distance before veering left and starting up an increasingly steep incline. Hedgerows flank the left side, and a stone wall the right.

On the other side of the stone wall, pasture slopes down to a small coniferous forest at the bottom and a stand of woods along the north side, composed mainly of Sycamore. Although this tree is not native to Ireland, it grows well here, and is used for flooring, furniture and turning, as well as shelter-belts.

Hilltop

At the top of the hill there is a large block of concrete, and just beyond this is a T-junction. The path to the right eventually winds up on the Lodge Road, which comes out on the main Castlebar Road farther on.

At the top of the hill near Attireesh

Turn left here if you want to remain on the Greenway. At this point you are high above the surrounding countryside, with a fine view over the Reek and Sheeffrey Mountains to the south, and Ben Nephin and the Nephin Beg Mountains to the north.

Ragged hedgerows flank the edges of the path, with rolling pastureland stretching out on either side. The path begins to go downhill here, descending all the way to the bottom at Attireesh, where it joins up with a driveway.

Staggered gate at Attireesh

Old railway bridge

Attireesh juncture

Attireesh

At this juncture there is a road going off to the left, back to the main Westport-Newport road (N59). You follow straight on along the driveway.

Through the line of conifer trees on your left you can see a raised grassy bank – this is the original railway line, which merges with the Greenway a little farther up.

To your right is a patchwork of grassy fields edged by

hedgerows, rolling up the sides of drumlins. You pass through a pair of beautiful old gateposts surmounted by pyramids and cross over a small stream. To your left, beneath the raised embankment, you will see the old arched stone railway bridge which the original track went over.

The path turns left here and climbs up through the first gate of the Greenway, which is staggered – that is, a wooden gate comes slightly more than halfway across the path from one side, and directly ahead another one comes across from the other side.

A sign to your left announces the way to Creggaunnahorna, about a kilometre (just over half a mile) farther on. This is the anglicised spelling of the Irish Carraig na hEorna, meaning 'Barley Rock', referred to locally as 'Barley Hill'. On the gate here is a sign indicating that horses are not allowed on the Greenway.

About halfway up the incline a sign on an old upright railway sleeper states: "Please note you are entering onto active farmland. A special thank you to the land owners who have facilitated this trail development and for allowing recreation users to pass through their lands on a permissive basis."

At the top there is a cattle grid over half the width of the path beside an open gate – Gate 2. Just before this the original train track merges with the Greenway, and continues straight on through a mix of scrub and trees, pastureland and a few houses.

The trees along here are mostly Ash, Hawthorn and Beech. Wildflowers are abundant along the verges of the path, including the cheerful Ox-eye Daisy, the short purple stubs of Self-heal and the delicate twining Tufted Vetch.

Butter on the Tracks

Stories abound of youths rubbing butter on the rails at Barley Hill. The gradient is one of the steepest along the track from Newport, and the locomotive coming from there would find it impossible to climb the greasy rails. The train would have to reverse almost all the way back to Newport and start again in order to gather enough momentum to make it up the slippery slope.

Wildlife

If the plants and trees along the Greenway can be considered to play a leading role, the animals are the largely unseen players. Birds and insects are the among the most likely to be spotted, but with a bit of luck you may see other animals as well.

Along the first part of the Greenway, from Westport to around Kilmeena, there is a mixture of woodland, hedgerows, grassy pastures and drumlins, which play host to a wide range of birds, insects and mammals.

Songbirds such as the Blackbird (Lon Dubh in Irish), Robin (Spideog), Pied Wagtail (Glasóg Shráide), Song Thrush (Smólach Ceoil), Dunnock (Dunnóg) and Wren (Dreolín) may be seen on the ground, searching for worms and insects. The Greenfinch (Glasán Darach), Goldfinch (Lasair Choille), Chaffinch (Rí Rua) and Bullfinch (Corcrán Coille), predominantly seed-eaters, can be found higher up, in vegetation and trees. The House Sparrow (Gealbhan Binne), a relative of the finches, may be seen nearer to towns and farm buildings.

Blue Tits (Meantán Gorm), Long-tailed Tits (Meantán Earrfhada) and Great Tits (Meantán Mór) can be heard twittering noisily in the hedgerows. The latter have a wide variety of calls and songs, with up to 57 different refrains. The Long-tailed Tit creates one of the most intricate nests of any bird in Ireland, composed of mosses woven together with spider-webs and covered with bits of lichen.

Another widespread bird is the Starling (Druid), which feeds on plants and animals in both fields and trees. Aside from its own characteristic calls, it will imitate other birds and sounds such as chain saws and car alarms!

Jackdaws (Cág) and Hooded Crows (Feannóg), with their raucous cries, and their cousins,

Starling © Philip Heron, CC BY-SA 3.0

Common Blue Butterfly

the chattering Magpies (Snag Breac), are also numerous throughout the area. They are omnivorous and will eat just about anything, including young birds and eggs. Rooks (Préachán dubh), another member of the crow family, can often be seen near towns in treetop colonies called rookeries.

Swifts (Gabhlán Gaoithe) and Barn Swallows (Fáinleog) can be seen swooping about in the sky. Swifts are dark all over with a grey throat and have scythe-shaped wings held straight out from the body, while swallows, about the same size, have unmistakable long tail-streamers and a white belly. These agile flyers subsist almost exclusively on insects caught on the wing. They are both migrant birds, only visiting our shores in the late spring and summer. They spend the winters in Africa.

The abundance of wildflowers and shelter along this section of the Greenway provides a good habitat for moths and butterflies. These beautiful creatures play an important role as pollinators and as a food source for birds, but they are greatly at risk from encroaching development.

Two of the most common butterflies you might see along here are the Common Blue (Gormán Coiteann) and the Speckled Wood (Breacfhéileacán Coille). A fairly small butterfly, the Common Blue male has iridescent lavender-blue upper wings, while the female is generally blue and brown. The butterfly has a curious relationship with ants. Its chrysalis is attended by the insects, which often take it into their anthill. The larva exudes a substance called honeydew that the ants eat without harming it. The Speckled Wood is dark brown with cream-coloured spots, which imitate dappled sunlight in woodlands. Males can be seen flying together in tight spirals, fighting over territory.

Many mammals, such as the Badger (Broc), Hedgehog (Gráinneog) and Pine Martin (Cat Crainn) are nocturnal and so are unlikely to be seen by most Greenway users. You may be lucky enough to catch a glimpse of other animals, such as the the Irish Stoat (Easóg), a beautiful creature with a long narrow body, which is deep reddish-brown above and creamy-white below, with a black tip on its long tail. It is very playful and inquisitive, but can also be ferocious. It will attack animals much larger than itself with a single, strong bite to the back of the neck.

You may also see the American Mink (Minc Mheiriceánac). In the same family as the Irish Stoat, it is not native but was originally released or escaped into the wild from fur farms and has adapted well to the Irish climate. It is much darker than the Stoat and can be found around the numerous streams in the area. It is a good swimmer and eats just about any kind of aquatic prey, but will also hunt water birds and other land mammals.

The Irish Hare (Giorria), which is quite large and stocky, can also be glimpsed occasionally. It is a very fast runner, and in the spring the males box in a pre-mating display.

The Rabbit (Coinín) is much smaller than the Hare and prefers areas of short grass near cover such as brambles and hedgerows. Hedgerows are important corridors for wildlife, acting as a sort of Greenway for animals and providing cover between nesting and feeding areas. Rabbits

Stoat © Peter Trimming, CC BY-AT 2.0

Long-eared Bat, by Ernst Haeckel, public domain

were introduced by the Normans in the 12th century so that their extensive underground warrens would provide a ready supply of game.

The Red Fox (Sionnach/Madra Rua), although primarily nocturnal, is sometimes spotted during the day. It is a good swimmer and can even climb trees. It is very territorial and marks its boundaries with a strong musky odour. During the mating season in January and February, the female (vixen) utters a piercing high-pitched cry, while both adults have a distinctive triple bark. Often they will mate for life. Although they can attack newborn sheep, they are more likely to scavenge dead sheep or lambs, and they help to keep crop-damaging rabbits and rodents under control.

If you are out at dusk you are more than likely to see bats, which flit through the air in search of insects. A Pipistrelle, weighing no more than a Euro coin, can consume up to 3,500 insects in one night, so they are a welcome controller of midges and mosquitos. Bats can see perfectly well, but they rely on echolocation for hunting. They are the only flying mammal, and there are nine species in Ireland. They can often be found roosting under bridges.

All of the amphibians and mammals mentioned above are protected under the Wildlife Act, with the exception of the American Mink, Fox, Mice, Rat and Rabbit. It is against the law to kill, injure or catch any of these protected species, and their breeding and resting places may not be damaged or disturbed even if there are no animals present. Only specific humane methods may be used in capturing or culling all other wild animals.

All birds, nests and eggs are also protected under the Wildlife Act. It is illegal to trap, injure or kill almost all birds or to disturb or damage their nests.

The track is elevated and commands fine views across rolling fields and tree-lines to Croagh Patrick in the distance.

Information Board

Presently you reach an old arched limestone bridge which carries the main road overhead. On the other side of this, wooded embankments rise up sharply on both sides, creating a deep shady glade. The trees here are older and mainly Ash; many are choked with Ivy.

Farther on there is a small clearing with the first of the many information boards dotted along the Greenway. This has an excellent map of the entire route, with details of the distances and times between various sections. Next to it is a very realistic bronze sculpture of antique suitcases, giving a flavour of travel in the last century and beyond.

Barley Hill

A short distance ahead you come to the arches of two more old overhead bridges of dressed limestone. The path climbs gently to an open spot next to a stockyard. Here the track departs from the main road and plunges through hedgerows elevated above grassy fields and pastureland. The trees along here are mainly Birch, Ash, Willow, Hawthorn and Holly.

Suitcase Sculptures

This sculpture and others in the same style dotted along the Greenway were created by Wicklow sculptor Tim Morris, who works out of his studio in Foxford.

They were designed with a playful spirit to evoke a time when travelers would toss their bags out of the train windows as they neared home. When they walked back from the station they could collect their luggage on the way and not have to carry it so far.

Elegant arched overhead bridge near Creggaunahorna

Eventually the surrounding land draws level with the track and begins to shoulder up above it again. On the east side some steps made of railway sleepers and gravel ascend to a small raised area with two wooden benches – a pleasant spot to stop for a moment and admire the kaleidoscope of blossoms that have been planted along the pathway here. Nearby are gates leading to private grounds, and a few of these also have bright patches of garden flowers decorating their entrances.

Soon after this the track passes through an open gate – Gate 3 – and emerges into open wet grassland. A little farther on it passes through Gate 4 (also open) and runs between a small stand of conifers by a large aluminium barn.

Here you pass through another open gate (Gate 5), and the track angles down to run alongside the main road. After a short distance it ducks behind a hedgerow again and once more runs between wooded embankments, parallel to the main road.

This is interrupted briefly by an elaborate gateway up to a large house to the west. Here you pass through Gate 6, which is spring-loaded.

The hedgerows draw in again, and the land levels out and then falls to either side. Wildflowers along here are abundant, with luxuriant carpets of Black Medick and Red Clover, pierced by Thistles and Himalayan Balsam.

Watercress

Below the high wooded embankments here are drainage ditches foaming with leafy green Watercress.

High in vitamin C, this has been a valued food down through the centuries and still is, although one must be careful not to eat watercress that has been contaminated with liver fluke, a consequence of water running off of fields with sheep on them.

In these parts in bygone days watercress was also rubbed on the skin to cure rashes and blemishes.

Himalayan Balsam

Himalayan Balsam is originally, as the name implies, from the western Himalayas. It was introduced to Britain in 1839 and found its way to Ireland.

A tall handsome plant, with clusters of pink or white helmet-shaped flowers, its seed pods spring apart at the slightest touch, enabling the plant to broadcast its copious seeds to a distance of 7m (22ft). It is considered invasive, as it can rapidly take over an area, especially along river banks, where it crowds out native species and causes erosion.

Collies

A little farther on you pass a livestock gate and then come to Gate 7, which is open. Just beyond it is a concrete-block livestock pen. The path continues much as before and eventually angles down to the main road again.

Here you pass across a driveway with two gateposts, each decorated with a charming painted statue of a collie. Beside the gates is a small field, beyond which is a well-tended vegetable patch.

Painted collie on gate-post

The path continues along the edge of the small field, separated from the road by just a strip of grass and a low wooden fence. It crosses over a small lane heading west and then passes through Gate 8, which is staggered.

A short distance ahead is Gate 9, also staggered. On the other side of this is another small lane heading northeast. Up the road a little way you can just glimpse a tiny railway cottage. This was originally where the gate-keeper for the level crossing here lived. It is still occupied and in mint condition.

On the other side of the lane is Gate 10, again staggered. This stretch passes beneath the railway cottage, which is perched on top of a high embankment to the western side.

A little farther along you come to a sinuous blue metal-railed bridge across the narrow Moyour River. Just to the west of this is a large ornamental pond in the lawn below a house, surrounded by a well-tended garden.

Buckfield

A short distance ahead is Gate 11, which is staggered, and on the other side of this is a road heading west to Buckfield. Across the road is Gate 12, also staggered, and beside this are the fenced-in ruins of another railway cottage which has been partially rebuilt. This was known as Whitegates, and there are plans to renovate it and install toilets for Greenway users.

On the other side of the gate, in the summertime, is a lush patch of Euphorbia like a fresh lime-green froth. You pass through a grove of mixed young trees, with glimpses of verdant fields and rolling hills off to the west.

Level Crossing Cottages

Between Westport and Achill there were 16 level crossings, and originally the crossing gates closed off the roads, leaving the track open.

A Crossing Keeper was kept at the busiest crossings and was provided with a small standard cottage. The keepers had to open and close the gates for traffic and keep the oil lamps on the gates lit. They were paid a modest salary, as they only worked when a train came through.

Kilgallán church in Kilmeena village

The name Kilgallán is from Cill, meaning 'church' and Gallán, meaning 'standing stone'. Originally a Church of Ireland chapel, it was built in 1836. In 1901 its bell tower was struck by lightening, causing such substantial damage that church services ceased to be held there.

It remained unused for a century, and at some point the roof was removed for tax purposes. The interior became overrun with plants and animals. Some years ago it was beautifully restored and is now rented out as a holiday home.

Kilgallán Church

The path takes an S bend and emerges from the trees to run alongside a farm. To the west, through a line of trees in the distance, you can catch a glimpse of the beautiful limestone Kilgallán Church in Kilmeena village

The path runs across a driveway right next to the road and is then separated from the traffic by a thin band of trees, with open pastureland off to the west. If you glance backwards you can catch a fine view of Croagh Patrick. The verges here are fringed with a colourful display of wildflowers.

Eventually you come to Gate 13, a single, open gate just before a wooden-railed bridge. The bridge crosses over a small stream which flows between Gorteen Lough to the east and the Moyour River to the south.

Immediately after this the path runs directly next to the main road for some distance, separated only by a low, thin concrete barrier. There are interesting gardens and houses on either side of the road along here, and eventually tree-covered embankments envelop you again.

Old railway bridge beside Greenway track

Kilmeena Church

Nearly blending in with the curved canopy of trees overhead is an old stone humpbacked bridge arching above the path. This leads from the main road to a large old house high up on the west embankment.

On the other side of the bridge is an information board, one of the few along this stretch of Greenway, and then Gate 14, a staggered gate on the edge of a busy side road signposted for Kilmeena Church and other destinations.

The track resumes a stone's throw down this road, zig-zagging along wooden fencing through a cover of trees. A ridge running parallel to the left or west side of the track indicates the original railway line, as evidenced farther on by an old stone bridge.

Crossing the main road

Kilmeena Crossroads

A chain-link fence runs alongside the entire length of this ridge, while on the other edge you are somewhat screened from traffic by a bank of vegetation. Eventually you come to a crossroads.

On the opposite side of the main road is the Kilmeena Community Centre. The side road, which you have to cross, signposted for Kilmeena, is extremely busy. It is impossible to see very far up it, so take extreme care in crossing here.

The path continues for a short distance on the other side, and then you come to stop signs. Here you must cross the main road. The speed limit along here is 100kph, though fortunately the visibility in both directions is very good. There are plans to improve this crossing in the near future.

Grotto and Celtic Cross

Once across the N59, the Greenway merges with a side road that runs parallel to the main road for a short distance. There

Kilmeena Ambush

The cross has an inscription in Irish and English, honouring the memory of the local men who died in the Kilmeena Ambush during the Irish War of Independence.

On the 19th of May 1921, the West Mayo Brigade of the IRA attacked a British convoy, consisting of about 50 men of the Royal Irish Constabulary and the Black and Tans, en route from Westport to Newport. The result was a shootout in which four IRA men were killed. One was badly wounded, as was one RIC man, both of whom died later on.

Another man from Newport was killed when the British pursued the fleeing IRA Brigade into the mountains. The British dumped the wounded and dead bodies of the IRA men in the street outside the RIC barracks in Westport, which outraged the local people.

Grotto of the Virgin Mary

are two points of interest here: an elaborately carved Celtic cross to the right, and to the left, a grotto of the Virgin Mary in her sky-blue robes standing atop a green snake.

A short distance beyond the grotto, the side road bends to the east while the Greenway continues on straight. It goes over a small rise between wooden fencing and drops down to Gate 15, which is staggered, though one side of it is open.

At the bottom of this the path is paved and travels on directly beside the main road. The east side is bordered by an impressive trimmed hedge of hawthorn with gently sloping fields beyond. Across the road are marshy lands and rolling hills.

Presently the path curves away from the road and tucks in behind a steep bank. Here the surface reverts to grit. Soon it veers back to run alongside the main road again, and presently comes to Gate 16, about knee-high and semi-staggered. Just past it is a small road heading east, and on the other side of this is Gate 17, also staggered.

Wet Grasslands

Beyond this the path curves away from the main road through flat damp fields and wildflowers. Soon you reach a sinuous blue-railed bridge across the Owennabrockagh River. You can still see the stone supports of the old railway bridge beneath the new one.

From here the path ducks behind a house shielded by a high wooden fence and winds through farmland, passing through open gates numbers 18 and 19. After Gate 19, you come to a humpbacked white-railed bridge over the Rossow River. Here the path turns from grit to graveled tarmacadam and follows the snaking river through open wet grass-

Wet grassland

land grazed by sheep, cattle and the odd donkey, and bordered by wildflowers.

Eventually the track passes through Gate 20, which is also open, and reverts to grit. Off to the left you can see the traces of a path that was laid down and then left unused. Instead, the track continues on straight until it merges with a private driveway, perpendicular to the track. Here you are directed to turn left. You follow the driveway until the Greenway veers off to the right and proceeds through Gate 21 onto a small laneway.

Croagh Patrick Seafoods

Across the fields to the west you can see a double-arched stone bridge. To the Newport side of it is a road which goes down to Rosbeg Peninsula. Half-way along this is Croagh Patrick Seafoods, another member of the Gourmet Greenway Trail.

The Gannon family harvests oysters, mussels and clams fresh from their mari-culture sites located close to their family farm. If you are interested in a tour, their website is www.croaghpatrickseafoods.ie.

Wildlife in Wet Grasslands

Wet grasslands such as these are important habitats for a wide variety of plants, insects and birds and provide breeding grounds for birds such as Snipe, Lapwing and Redshank. Compared to most other habitats, they contain a denser population of wading birds, which feed at the edges of pools and probe the soft damp soil for insects.

Grey Herons (Corr Réisc in Irish) can often be seen standing stock-still, ready to strike at a passing fish with their spear-like beak. They are our largest wading birds at 1m (3.3ft) tall, with long necks and an impressive wingspan of 185cm (6ft). They will also take frogs, lizards, insects and small mammals.

Redshanks (Cosdeargán) are smaller birds, recognisable by their long bright-red legs. Some are resident, while others are migratory. They usually feed in large flocks for safety.

Lapwings (Pilibín), medium-sized waders, are found here mainly in winter, gathering in large flocks. They have a conspicuous dark wispy crest, an iridescent purple-green back, rounded wings, and a white belly and throat with a black breast band. Their call is a plaintive 'pee-wit'.

Snipe (Naoscach) can be hard to spot, as they are well camouflaged in the reeds and rushes. When flushed, they are easily identifiable by their very long, straight bills and zig-zag pattern of flight, accompanied by a repeated rasping cry. In springtime they fly methodically over their nesting sites calling loudly, then suddenly dive down with an eerie sound like a goat bleating. This noise is referred to as 'drumming' and is produced by the rapid vibration of stiff feathers sticking out of the sides of the tail.

Small Copper butterfly © Evelyn Simak, CC BY-SA 2.0

The Common Frog (Loscán) and the Common Newt (Earc Sléibhe) also abound here. Frogs can change colour to match their surroundings

Lapwing © Hans Hillewaert, CC BY-SA 3.0

but are generally yellow-brown, grey, green or even russet, with a pattern of dark markings on the back and a brown patch behind each eye. The Common Newt is only 10cm (4 inches) long and olive green or pale brown with a speckled back and an orange belly. The only other amphibian in Ireland is the Natterjack Toad, found primarily in Kerry and parts of Wexford.

Two butterflies you are likely to spot are the Small Copper (Copróg Bheag) and the Orange Tip (Barr Buí). The Small Copper has bright copper forewings and can often be found resting on the ground or flowers with wings outstretched to soak up the sun. The males of the Orange Tip are white with bright orange wing-tips. Their larvae feed on Lady's Smock, abundant here in springtime.

Orange Tip butterfly

Properly managed seasonal grazing can enhance the botanical richness of wet grasslands, as grazing and trampling can provide niches for the regeneration of plants.

Beyond the Wetlands

Here you turn left again and follow the lane down to where the track resumes off to the right, by a compound enclosed by spiked green fencing. There is an ever-changing kaleidoscope of interesting artifacts behind the fencing, including classic cars, ancient tractors, an antique threshing machine and a collection of old brightly-coloured tractor seats.

Just in front of this, the track goes over a very small wooden-railed bridge across a tiny stream and then passes through Gate 22, which is open. You pass across two driveways and then through Gate 23, which is staggered but half-open.

A short distance on, you come to another small road heading east from the main road. You turn right and follow the small road for a short distance, then turn left onto the Greenway again. In late summer this stretch blazes with stunning colour; just to the right of the entrance here is a clump of bright red Poppies, while the strip of wetlands to the other side is a solid mass of Purple Loosestrife.

A private driveway parallels the track here, and all along it you can get glimpses of quirky objects, such as bicycles hanging from tree branches, an old boat, and sculptural arrangements of natural unusual-shaped stones mingled with random objects.

Display of old tractor seats in compound

The original railway line went along here; you can still see the small arched bridge crossing a small stream beside the Greenway. A belt of Willow and Ash mixed with conifers runs along between the old and new tracks.

The bright hues of Purple Loosestrife

Presently this transforms into a grassy embankment, while on the other side the land falls away to wet grasslands. Farther along, the embankment levels out into scrubland, which soon gives way to a new verge which has been planted with various saplings, Yellow Flag Iris and red Poppies.

New Section

Initially the Greenway stopped at this point, and pedestrians and cyclists were obliged to use the roadway into Newport. Now it follows on along the original railway track which ran directly beside the road.

A flat stretch of wet grasslands extends away to the east, giving way to scrub as it scrambles up a steep drumlin. The verges are festooned with Queen Anne's Lace, Daisies, Knapweed and Tufted Vetch.

Soon you come to a small road heading eastward. On the other side of this a thicket of Willow and Hawthorn stands with its toes in the water, and beyond this is another expanse of wet grassland. If you look back you can catch a glimpse of Broad Lough glimmering behind the trees.

Kilbride Cemetery

You cross a second side-road heading east and there is a holy well a short way down this on the left-hand side. Before long you come to a third laneway, which goes down to Kilbride Cemetery.

Railway Tunnel

Soon after the lane to the cemetery, a steep bank rises to the east side of the path. Across the road you will see signs pointing west for an Art Gallery and Rossanrubble.

Queen Anne's Lace

Queen Anne's Lace, or Wild Carrot (*Daucus carota*), is a relative of the cultivated carrot. As it grows, its umbels become concave, resembling a miniature bird's nest.

In fact, starlings like to use material from this plant to line their nests, and, amazingly enough, it contains the steroid B-sitosterol, which is fatal to fowl mites. It is a host plant to the Swallowtail caterpillar, and its nectar attracts many butterflies, bees and beneficial insects.

A short distance ahead there is another road to the west, while to the east you will see a driveway which passes between a break in the fencing. This is where the railway track departed from the road and ran through the first of two stone tunnels into the town of Newport.

Eventually it is hoped that the Greenway will pass through these two tunnels and connect up with the viaduct in Newport. For the moment it continues along beside the main road, passing a petrol station and a tennis court, to join up with a footpath which brings you into the town and across the river.

Kilbride Ambush

This area was the scene of an ambush in November 1922. After the Irish War of Independence, Ireland was split politically between the Free Staters, who supported the Anglo-Irish Treaty, and those who did not accept it. Civil war erupted.

On the night of the 23rd of November three members of the West Mayo Brigade of the Irish Volunteers learned that an advance party of the Free State troops had slipped through an IRA column positioned in Kilmeena and were advancing on Newport.

The Volunteers raced to take up a position at Kilbride, and when the Free State soldiers arrived, they opened fire. The soldiers took cover and responded with heavy machine gun fire, and soon the three men were unable to maintain their ground.

General Michael Kilroy, one of the three, left the other two to fend off the soldiers and ran a considerable distance around to the other side of them, where he resumed shooting until he could no longer withstand their heavy return fire. He retreated towards the railway line, where he was wounded and captured.

Four Free State soldiers were killed that night and a number wounded. General Kilroy was subsequently imprisoned in Mountjoy Jail.

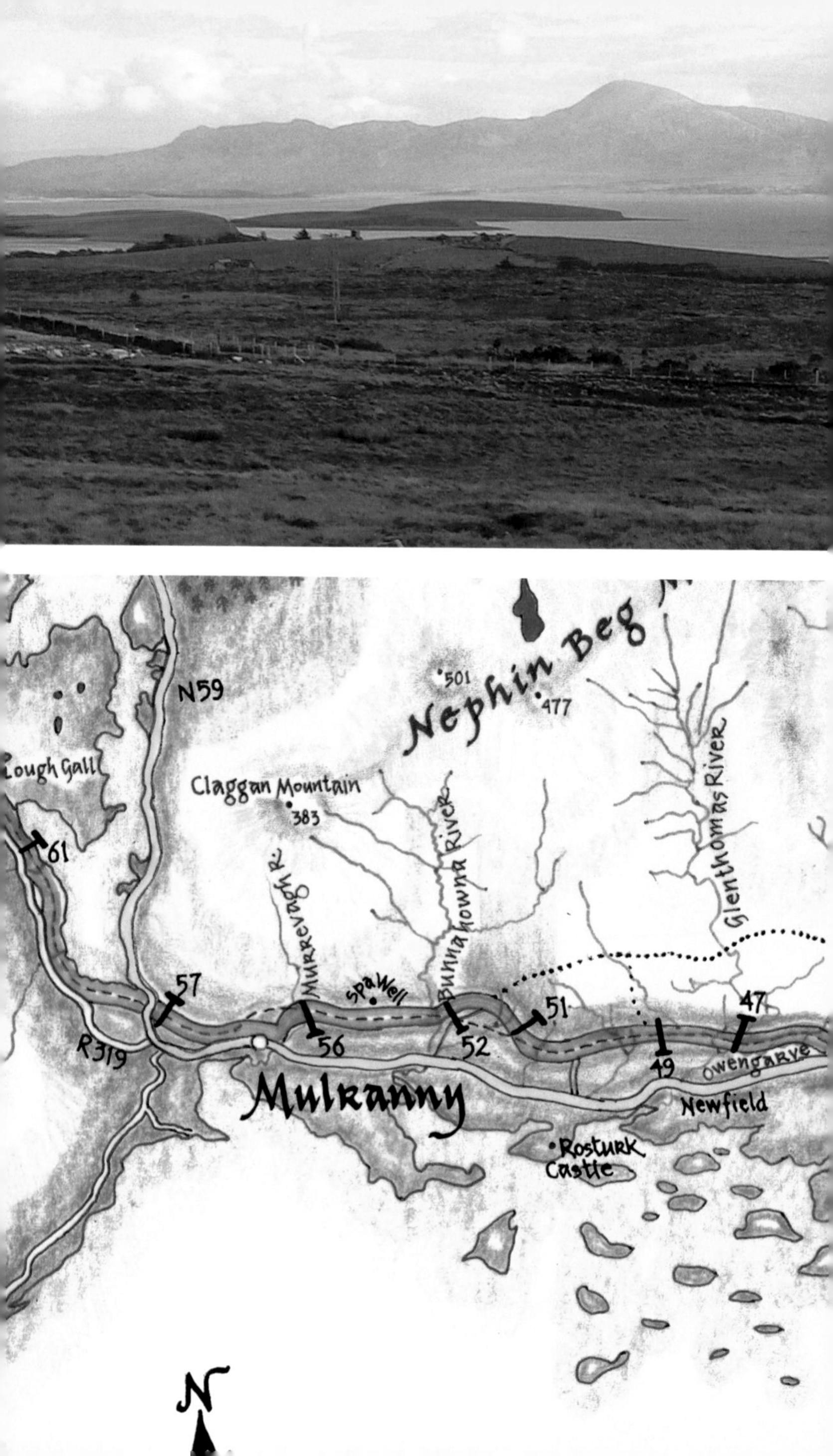
Nephin Beg
501
477
N59
Lough Gall
Claggan Mountain
383
Murrevagh R.
Bunnahowna River
Glenthomas River
61
57
spa Well
56
52
51
49
47
R319
Owengarve
Mulranny
Newfield
Rosturk Castle
N

Newport to Mulranny

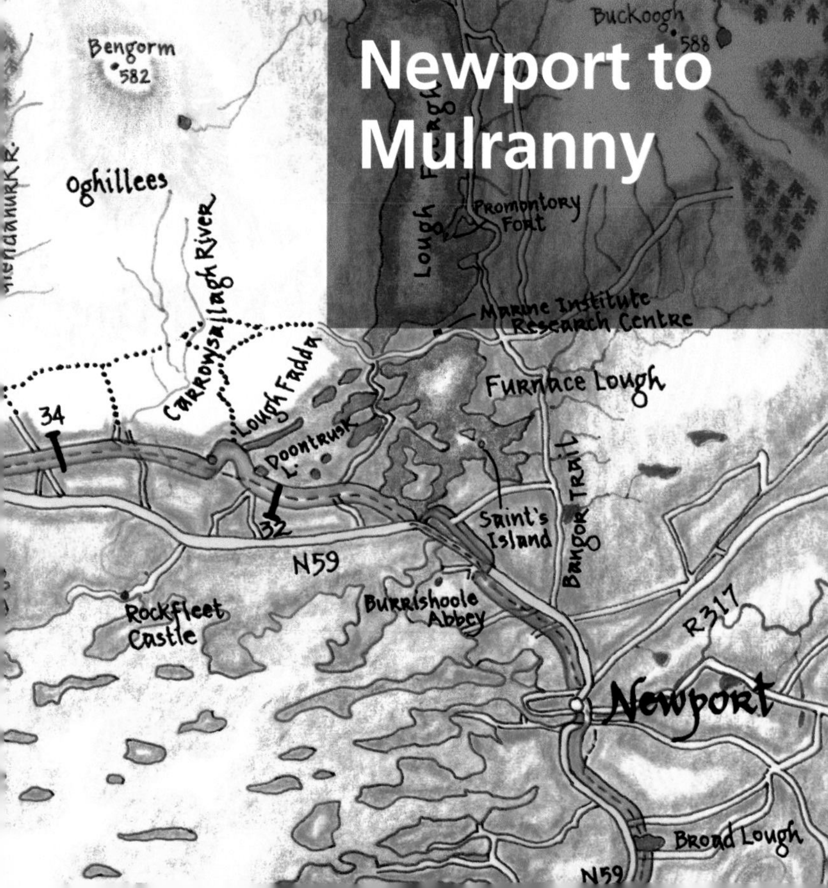

In a Nutshell

The distance from **Newport to Mulranny** is 18km (11 miles). The estimated cycling time is 2-2½ hours, while walking should take from 5-5½ hours at a good pace.

Except for a short section starting out from Newport, this part of the Greenway is very peaceful, being far removed from the main road. It runs along the beautiful Burrishoole River, across the old seven-arched bridge, and along Lough Furnace. It passes through open fields and woodlands, bordered by drifts of wildflowers for much of the way.

Two old railway cottages feature along the way, as well as several ruined houses. Eventually you encounter open bogland, pass by a few more lakes, over several small rivers, and through rich verges of wildflowers.

The old ford across the Owengarve River is a sight not to be missed. Along one of the cuttings you will see a rock with an old bore hole where dynamite was used to open up the track.

There is a small stretch which is a bit rougher and steeper than the rest of the Greenway, where the path takes a substantial departure from the original track; the views across the landscape and sea are stunning along here.

Farther on you come to the dramatic sandstone bridge across the Bunnahowna River, and then the mysterious high sandstone walls stretching as far as the eye can see. Another interesting feature nearby is the Spa Well beside the track. Spectacular views of Clew Bay open up as you near the end of this segment at Mulranny.

There are several loop walks intersecting with this section of the Greenway. They are all part of the Burrishoole Loop Walks, of which there are 12 in four different areas: Newport, Derrada, Tiernaur and Mulranny.

They are of varying degrees of ease or challenge and range from 3km (1.9 miles) to 16km (10 miles). All are marked with different coloured arrows.

You can get the brochures on these walks from Newport Tourist Office, or you can download them from the web at www.mayowalks.ie/WalkingTrails/LocalisedLoopWalks/BurrishooleLoops.

Newport's Setting

Black Oak River

The approach to Newport is quite spectacular. The town is dominated by the magnificent seven-arched viaduct spanning the Newport, or Black Oak River, which flows through the centre of Newport into a tidal estuary.

This tidal area provides a habitat for fish nurseries and a home for shellfish and marine invertebrates, which are food sources for wildfowl and wading birds such as the Curlew, Redshank and Heron.

The Newport River is host to Shrimp, Salmon, Sea Trout and Brown Trout, as well as the Fresh-water Pearl Mussel, which used to be widely hunted for its pearls. This mussel has a life span of up to 130 years and relies on water of the purest quality; in parts of Europe it has become extinct. The Newport River is a Special Area of Conservation and one of two designated catchment areas in Mayo for this critically endangered mussel, which is afforded a high level of protection.

The river also supports some other interesting species. Leisler's Bat (Ialtóg Leisler in Irish), which is often associated with water, can be found skimming up and down the river at dusk.

The Kingfisher (Cruidín) with its colourful, jewel-like plumage can sometimes be seen perched beside the river, motionlessly waiting for a fish to appear. Diving head-first, it spears the fish with its dagger-like beak.

The Long-eared Owl (Ceann Cait) has also been recorded around Newport. This is a beautiful owl with striking orange eyes, a russet facial disc and two prominent tufts on the head, which are not actually ears, but feathers. They are nocturnal hunters, preying on small mammals, frogs and other birds.

Viaduct

The dramatic viaduct was built in the late 1800s to carry the train from Westport to Achill across the river, and is now pedestrianised. It is built of local red sandstone with limestone facings.

If you stand at the south end of the viaduct and look past the stone building on the other side of the street, you can just make out the old tunnel in the hill behind it. As mentioned earlier, there were originally two tunnels coming into Newport, but they are now overgrown and inaccessible.

Church

A much lower stone bridge for vehicular traffic spans the river to the west of the viaduct. Above it, to the north, towers the fine Roman Catholic church of St. Patrick. This was built in 1914 in the Irish Romanesque style, and is well worth a visit; the majestic eastern window, depicting the Last Judgement, was the last window created by the famous stained-glass artist Harry Clarke.

Just below the church is the old Newport railway station, now council offices, and next to it is the old storehouse, which has been turned into a small chapel.

Harry Clarke stained-glass windows in St. Patrick's Church

Gourmet Trail

Out on the Main Street are a hotel and a number of pubs, cafes and shops, including Kelly's Butchers, which is listed as a member of the Gourmet Greenway Trail, and which has won many prizes for black and white puddings. Their website is: www.kellysbutchers.com.

Newport House is also a member of the Gourmet Trail. Treat yourself to a special experience by visiting this fine, historic Georgian house, where you can dine in style. Fresh seafood is sourced there daily, and they smoke their own salmon. There is a full bar and a comprehensive wine list. You can also visit them on the web at www.newporthouse.ie.

Tourist Office

The tourist office, located on Georges Street in the old grain-drying store, is also well worth a visit. Behind the main office is a room with arched ceilings and walls that were designed to convey the heat from a central fireplace up through the stone ceiling to dry the corn (grain) spread on the floor in the room above. It also contains a small museum.

Mural

While you are there, you can pick up a leaflet about the mural at the top of Georges Street. This fine mural depicts the story of Father Manus Sweeney, who was born in Rossmore, Newport in 1736. He was educated and ordained in Paris and returned to Newport, where he was appointed curate.

When the French came to Mayo in 1798 to assist the Irish in their rebellion against British rule, Fr Sweeney acted as an interpreter for the French captain. He was imprisoned in Newport House for this misdemeanor, but was later released. He became further involved in the Rebellion, and when that met with failure, he was captured and condemned to death for treason. He was hanged in Newport in 1799 and is buried at Burrishoole Abbey.

Music

On a more cheerful note, if you're looking for traditional music, there are several pubs in the town, including the

The Bangor Trail

Roughly 1km (0.6 miles) along the N59 west from Newport, a road off to the north (right), is the start of the Bangor Trail, which crosses northwest through the Nephin Beg Mountain Range, to Bangor. It is a challenging but wildly beautiful walk and dates back to at least the Iron Age. It crosses blanket bog, woodland, streams and rugged terrain.

For more information on this, read Mayo County Council's *A West of Ireland Walk Guide: County Mayo – The Bangor Trail,* by Joe McDermott and Robert Chapman.

Gráinne Uaile pub near the Post Office, which has one of the best sessions in Mayo every Thursday night throughout much of the year.

Another member of the Gourmet Greenway Trail, this traditional pub has been in the hands of the McManamon family for over a century. Fresh locally-sourced food is served here in a cosy atmosphere. Their website is www.grainneuailenewport.ie.

Out from Newport

In Newport there are footpaths along the route through the centre of town. Keep going straight through town, following the N59, which bears left towards Mulranny just past the bicycle hire shop (Newport Cycle Hire & Repairs).

The footpath follows along the south (or left) side of the N59, and a short distance along this, you will see a big sign for the Greenway. At this point the path leaves the road and

Gorse

Gorse (Aiteann in Irish), also known as furze or whin, is commonplace throughout Ireland. There are two types, one of which blooms in autumn, winter and spring (*Ulex europaeus*) and the other in late summer (*Ulex gallii*).

They are both spiky bushes with pea-like bright yellow flowers which exude a heady scent of coconut. At one time their crushed spines were used as fodder for cattle. The flowers are edible and have also been used to make tea and wine. They are nitrogen-fixing plants and can thrive in poor soil, helping other plants to establish themselves. Birds also find the protective spines of gorse a good place to nest.

climbs up an incline. Along here the track is elevated above the road and runs through scrub and gorse.

Eventually the track comes level with the main road and passes a housing estate. After this it ducks behind an embankment separating it from the road and runs through more scrub. After a while you intersect a side road heading south towards an inlet from the sea. This leads to Burrishoole Abbey, well worth a visit.

Road crossing

Road Crossing

At the top of the road down to Burrishoole Abbey, you must cross the main road to the other side. The visibility here is good in both directions but take care in crossing, as the speed limit is 100kph (62mph).

There are plans to improve this crossing in the near future. This part of the main road used to be the railway track, while the original main road followed what is now signposted as the Greenway.

On the north side of the road, a sign points to your left, or west, towards "Mallarany," or, as most people around here both spell and pronounce it, Mulranny. Mallarany was the spelling consistently used by the railway.

The trail passes Reek View B&B, surrounded by a cheerful display of colourful flowers, and runs parallel to the small side road here. After a short distance the track and road merge. This quiet laneway used to be the main road. It gradually veers away from the present-day main road, passing by fields, trees and a few houses.

Sandstone

As you head west from Newport, you may begin to notice more structures built with a reddish stone. The geological composition of this coastal region, as far as Mulranny, is mainly lower carboniferous sandstone. It is durable and yet relatively soft, making it easy to cut.

Burrishoole River

Presently the waters of the Burrishoole River sparkle into sight to the southwest, affording a good view of the modern-day road bridge crossing over it. This was originally the railway bridge.

Farther along this road there is a turn to the right or north, but you stay on the present road and follow the signpost with the symbol of a bicycle, pointing straight ahead. Watch out for traffic here. A short distance ahead, off to the south on your left, you will see a beautiful old limestone bridge with seven arches spanning the Burrishoole River.

Burrishoole River

Along the river here is a wide stretch of tidal marshland, an area rich in plant and bird life. Worms, crustaceans and shellfish in the mud provide abundant food for wild fowl, wading birds and otters, while the river bottom serves as a fish nursery.

As the seawater extends all the way up to Lough Furnace during spring tides (the most extreme tides following full and new moons), there is a vast diversity of wildlife throughout this area, forming an important conservation resource.

This is an especially good place to spot Otters (Dobharcú/Dobhrán in Irish), which are found along the many streams in the area, especially under bridges and other spots which provide cover. Otters also frequent the coastline, but they require fresh water to wash their coats in order to maintain their insulating properties.

Otters are rather awkward on land, with a humped, loping gait, but are superb acrobats in the water, and they are very playful. Keep an eye out for their droppings (spraints), which contain crab shells and fish scales and bones, and are left on prominent rocks and ledges as a means of marking their territory.

They are rare in the rest of Europe; hence our otter population is of international importance.

Burrishoole Abbey

According to the Office of Public Works sign at the Abbey, "All that remains today is the church and the eastern wall of the cloister in which the monks walked and meditated. All the domestic buildings – the kitchen, the dormitories, and the refectory (dining hall) – have been destroyed. The church consists of a nave and chancel, a south transept and a low tower."

Technically this was not an abbey but a Dominican Friary, as the order did not have abbots. It was built in the 15th century by Richard de Burgo of Turlough, who resigned his title of Lord MacWilliam Oughter in 1469 to enter the friary, where he lived until his death in 1473. It contained dormitories, cloisters, a refectory, a church with a bell tower and a cemetery.

The friary was dissolved by Henry VIII during the Reformation in the 16th century. A century later it was used as a Cromwellian garrison for a time.

Nevertheless, the friary thrived until the 17th century, when many friars left Ireland. Others moved into cottages nearby, and in 1793 the roof of the friary collapsed. The last friar of Burrishoole wore the habit in the 1860s.

Burrishoole was originally known as Ceann Trachta, meaning "the head of the strand." Even before the first Norman family, the Butlers, invaded the area in 1185, Burrishoole was a port of some significance. It could accommodate a ship of 500 tonnes at low tide.

To quote from Nicholas Malbie in 1579, from H.T. Knox, *The History of County Mayo, 1908*: "It hath a goodly and large lough on the upper part of the river, full of great timber, grey marble, and many other commodities of all sides, not without great store of good ground, both arable land and pasture. Specially it hath a very plentiful iron mine and abundance of wood every way... there cometh hither every year likely and fifty English ships for fishing...."

Ships from places such as Spain, Portugal and England came here to trade for barrels of salted fish, oak staves and stone. Risteárd an Iarainn Bourke, or 'Iron Richard', of Rockfleet Castle, had an iron works here, lending the name Furnace to the lake upriver.

A little farther on you will come to a picturesque cottage on your right, and here the road bends sharply to the south and crosses over the old stone bridge.

Once across the bridge, you need to follow the small Greenway signs very carefully. You first take a sharp right, followed by a sharp left through Gate 24 (the first gate out from Newport). The road itself carries on to the right, along the river, and then turns south, under a bridge. Again, this is part of what used to be the main road.

The Bridges of Burrishoole

Built in the 18th century on the site of a ford dating back to the 13th century, this seven-arched bridge originally carried the main road between Newport and Mulranny.

At the end of the 19th century the railway bridge was built a short distance downriver, but in 1950 the rails were lifted and the bridge was widened for automobile traffic, and this became the main thoroughfare.

By the early 1990s the salt air had corroded the steel sections of the original railway bridge so badly that its deck had to be replaced. While this was being carried out, the seven-arched stone bridge again became the main road until work was completed.

Original railway bridge, now road bridge, with statue on right

Sister Honoria

Amidst the dark pine trees on the far side of the bridge gleams the stark white grotto of the Virgin Mary.

There is an inscription on the stone beneath her in Irish. One story about this goes that in the days of Cromwell, a band of British soldiers attacked the cloister near Burrishoole Friary. One of the nuns, Sister Honoria, who was the daughter of 'Iron Richard', himself the second husband of Grace O'Malley (Granuaile), escaped from the cloister. Some soldiers set off in pursuit and when they were almost upon her, they suddenly found themselves cut off by a stream which instantly sprang up and formed an island around her as she prayed. (Some cynics say the tide came in!)

Other stories say that Sister Honoria was quite elderly when the Cromwellian troops attacked the cloister around 1653. She fled to Saint's Island in Lough Furnace, but was captured by the soldiers. Another nun, a McGann, hid in a wood nearby, but was found soon afterwards dead of exposure. Sister Honoria reputedly lived to the age of 104!

Once through the gate, the path rises slightly, and at the top of the incline you will come to a picnic table and an information board with a map of the Greenway.

Gate 24, on Mulranny side of Burrishoole Bridge

Just a little farther along you will see a platform on your right, constructed of old railway sleepers. This is an excellent spot from which to view the lovely Burrishoole River and the old humpbacked bridge which you have just crossed. Just beyond the platform is a curvy red-railed footbridge crossing over the original main road below.

From here the track runs straight for a good distance and is flanked on either side by profuse colourful borders of wildflowers. In late summer, these mainly consist of Queen Anne's Lace, Ragwort, Wild Angelica, Thistles and Knapweed, with Ox-eye Daisies in the more open areas.

Border of wildflowers

Burrishoole and Greenway Bridges

Lough Furnace

As you pass through Gate 25, which is open, the woodland starts to close in, and the borders change to delicate white sprays of Enchanter's Nightshade mixed with the tiny bright pink blossoms of Herb Robert.

Bench with Birches by Lough Furnace

Up ahead you can see a glint of Lough Furnace through the trees. Graceful Birches overhang the pathway, which divides around an enchanting stand of Silver Birches arching over a wooden bench, well-positioned for travelers to sit upon and gaze out across the reed-plumed waters of Lough Furnace.

Woodland

From the bench by the lake, the pathway heads into dense scrubby woodland, with a narrow verge of grass and wildflowers. The trees through here are a mixture of fairly young Hawthorn, Birch, Beech, Hazel, Alder, Willow and Sycamore.

Lough Furnace

The Burrishoole River flows south from Lough Furnace, home of the Burrishoole Fisheries run by the Marine Institute. This extensive research unit has constructed two fish traps on the small rivers connecting Lough Furnace and Lough Feeagh, just to the north, which allow them to monitor the movements of Salmon, Sea Trout and Eels to and from fresh water. While the lake is used for scientific research, a small amount of fishing is permitted.

Lough Furnace is one of the few permanently stratified lakes in Ireland. It retains a dense layer of salt water on the bottom which ebbs and flows with the tide, overlain by a lighter layer of fresh water above. A wide range of fauna and invertebrates is sustained by this unusual habitat. One of the small islands in the lake, Saints Island, is used for nesting by Black-headed Gulls.

Here you may see Dragonflies and Damselflies hovering above the water or darting after insects. Dragonflies are strong and acrobatic fliers; whereas Damselflies are more delicate and fly only short distances. While their offspring, called "nymphs," spend up to four years in the water, the adults live for only a few weeks in summer.

You are also likely to spot Mute Swans floating along majestically or resting on the shore. They have orange-red bills with a prominent knob. They can often be seen with their heads under water and their rears tilted up in the air as they reach their long necks down to feed on aquatic plants.

They also graze on land and will sometimes supplement their diet with amphibians, snails and insects.

Diarmuid and Gráinne's Bed

Lough Feeagh is to the north of Lough Furnace and feeds into it through small rivers. The Marine Institute has set traps to monitor the movement of Salmon, Sea Trout and Eels.

Lough Feeagh is about twice as big as Lough Furnace and features what is thought to be a promontory fort on its east side, called Diarmuid and Gráinne's Bed.

It is built on a narrow spur sticking out into the lake and consists of what appears to be a double rampart of stone with a Chevaux de Frise, similar to the one flanking Dun Aengus on Inis Mór in the Aran Islands. This is a defensive construction of boulders and shafts of rock positioned in such a way as to impede access.

Lios na Gaoithe Ring-fort

The Bangor Trail passes along both of these lakes and proceeds north into Letterkeen Woods, where you can take another Loop Walk. There are several different trails through the woods, with varying degrees of difficulty.

Nearby is Lios na Gaoithe ring-fort, which means "Fort of the Wind." This consists of a raised bank of about 4m (13ft) in a circular shape with a diameter of roughly 26m (85ft).

It is believed to have been constructed in the late Iron Age and was probably an enclosure for a clan's homestead. It would have had wooden stakes positioned around the perimeter to protect the dwellers and their animals.

It is estimated that there are around 40,000 ring-forts scattered across the country. During excavations in 1950, a burial cist was found here, with the bones of the deceased and a number of blue glass beads, possibly from Africa, a sign that these ring-fort dwellers engaged in trading.

Straight 'tunnel' through trees

The path runs straight through the trees like a tunnel, and passes through Gate 26, which is open.

Gradually the woodland begins to thin out, and you come to a ruined sandstone cottage on your left, through a farm gate, with rolling rough fields beyond. A little farther on you come to another bench just before Gate 27, where the path narrows to a cattle grid.

Here the land opens out into cultivated fields sloping away to the north and uphill to the south, with views of Lough Furnace and the Nephin Beg mountains behind you to the east. This mountain range has been designated a Special Area of Conservation, and covers an area of 260km^2 (162 square miles).

A thin line of trees closes in again, the path takes a bend, and you come to Gate 28, also with a cattle grid. At the bend you can see where the original track went straight on, and indeed, a little farther along you come to a very small arched stone bridge down to the right side of the trail. Clearly, the old track continued straight on across the top of this bridge.

Old stone bridge

Railway View Cottage

Derrada

The path then passes through banks of wildflowers; in late summer you are surrounded by the bright orange of Montbresia, the cheerful yellow of Goldenrod and Ragwort, the soft lavender of Creeping Thistle and the smouldering purple-blue of Tufted Vetch. A slight downward incline takes you through Gate 29, which is half-open.

Here you emerge onto a narrow road. Attached to the wooden gatepost are signs for toilets, pointing down the road to the south towards Derrada Community Centre. This was originally the old National School and was in use for half a century. Today it is a popular venue for set dancing.

In the other direction, just on the edge of the road which carries on north up to Lough Furnace, is a tiny railway cottage, again originally the quarters for the individual who operated a level crossing here. The gate beside the house is crowned by a charming painted metal cutout of a train above the words "Railway View."

Across the road you re-enter the Greenway by a long high wooden fence, skirting along an old whitewashed cottage. Opposite it is a lower, horizontal fence, with many saplings planted behind it.

Greenway Farm

Also nearby is Colin and Alison McMullen's Greenway Farm, where fresh, organic vegetables and fruit are produced for local restaurants and markets.

Ducks, hens and geese are kept to provide free-range eggs. The farm is a member of the Gourmet Greenway Trail, and you can stop by on certain days or arrange a visit by emailing colinmcmullen@eircom.net.

Wildflowers along the verge

Ruined Cottages

The road curves a bit going between the wooden fences and then straightens out. A short distance along, you come to Gate 30, and beyond that smooth pastureland stretches out on both sides. It slopes up to the north and is dotted with a few trees and old ruined cottages.

Presently you arrive at Gate 31; in the summertime, passing through this is like stepping into an enchanted world. Here both verges of the pathway are awash with a foamy white tide of Queen Anne's Lace, flecked with violet-red Knapweed and Clover and the bright yellow heads of Ragwort, gradually mingling with tufts of brilliant magenta Bell Heather and Purple Loosestrife.

In the distance, beyond the green fields dotted with ruined cottages, loom the blue slopes of Bengorm in the Nephin Beg Mountains. The road curves a bit here, and suddenly the full range of wild, wind-swept bog and mountain tumbles into view.

Nephin Beg Mountains

The Mulchrone cottage

Ruined Cottages

According to local man Tommy Hughes, the first cottage belonged to the Mulchrone family, who lived their days out here. Close by is another small cottage which belonged to the O'Malleys. They moved out into a better house nearby in the first half of the 20th century.

The next house, which has a hipped roof, belonged to the Davitts, who emigrated to England in the first part of the last century. A hipped roof has a central ridge from which the four sides slope down to the top of each wall. The design was brought to Ireland by the Anglo-Normans during the Middle Ages.

It is more complicated to construct than a plain gable roof, but it makes the walls of the house easier to build, as the tops of them are all on the same level. Originally these roofs would have been thatched, and as the shape is more aerodynamic than a gable roof, it is better suited to strong winds. This house was probably constructed in the late 1800s or early 1900s.

The last cottage was owned by the Gormans, who also emigrated, probably to seek work and escape the poverty of their surroundings. One returned from England but settled in Newport, never returning to the cottage.

Railway Cottage

Railway cottage

For the moment, however, you are still surrounded by pastureland, somewhat rough and damp, but grazed by sheep and cattle. Across the green fields to the south you can glimpse a tiny picturesque railway cottage.

Presently you arrive at Gate 32. Just to the north is the small round glimmer of Doontrusk Lough. From here the trail bends left, towards the southwest, and forms a T-junction with a small lane that passes the tiny railway cottage. The original railway track continued straight on here, joining up with the Greenway farther along.

Lough Fadda

You turn right onto the lane, and follow it up to the southwest corner of Lough Fadda. This long sliver of a lake is true to its name, which in Irish (fada) means 'long'. (Fada is also the accent above a vowel in Irish.)

Along here is a rough road heading east along the north side of Doontrusk Lough. This is one of the Burrishoole

Lough Fadda

Picnic Table

Loop walks, and if you follow this it will bring you back to the old railway cottage near Derrada.

A short distance along from here the road forks by Lough Fadda. Follow the sharp turn to the left, or west, where there is a picnic table. The other arm goes up into the foothills of Bengorm (part of the Nephin Beg Range) and forms part of the Burrishoole Loop called Oghillies, named after an area of the mountain slopes to the north. You follow the tarmacadamed road which rises fairly steeply here, and a short way along it terminates at a small house on the right.

From here, the path reverts back to grit and continues

Viviparous Lizard

The Viviparous Lizard can sometimes be spotted on this type of boggy terrain, sunning itself on stones or dry hummocks of heather.

Our only native land reptile, it is an ectotherm, having no internal means of regulating body temperature.

The male, about 13cm (5 inches) in length, is shorter than the female, which ranges up to 20cm (8 inches). Both are covered with coarse scales and are usually a pale yellow-brown, dappled with irregular black tracings, though colour can vary somewhat according to their surroundings.

The name "viviparous" means bearing live young. The lizard's eggs develop within the mother and hatch inside her, so that the young emerge as free-living reptiles. In our cool climate, this is the only way for the animal to keep the eggs at a constant warm temperature.

slightly downhill to the south, passing across a short stretch of marshland. On the other side of this, you encounter Gate 33, and then the path rises again and turns to the west. This is the continuation of the original railway track.

Lough Stirkeen

Here the path runs straight for a long way, passing just south of Lough Stirkeen, which is of a similar size and shape to Doontrusk Lough.

Yarrow, Ox-eye Daisies and Thistles

The track is somewhat raised here, with rough and fairly boggy land to either side. In late summer, the verges are frothed with white Yarrow, Ox-eye Daisies and snowy drifts of thistledown, amongst which Linnets hop, picking at the seeds.

Carrowsallagh River

Presently you reach a sinuous green-railed footbridge, which passes across a small stream. You can still see the old stonework of the original bridgework on either side.

Bridge across the Carrowsallagh River

The path continues on much as before, plunging between abundant borders of wildflowers. After a while you come to a second green-railed bridge twisting high above the narrow Carrowsallagh River, which tumbles along a small ruined settlement half-hidden in a stand of trees to the north.

A little farther along this stretch two species of wildflowers can be found in late summer that are not seen much in other sections of the Greenway – clumps of short-petaled daisy-like flowers called Sneezewort and the angular stalks of delicate pink-flowered Centaury. Interestingly, both of these plants were used for stomach complaints in traditional medicine.

Ruins at Carrowsallagh

Gooseberry Jam

According to Dominick O'Grady, who lives nearby, there was once a lovely cottage here, inhabited by a couple named Hoban. It had a galvanised roof and was always nicely painted. There were a few cowsheds next to it.

The Hobans reached their house by a path that went underneath the railway bridge and is still visible today. A donkey and cart could just fit along here.

There were big granite flags in front of the house down the river. Dominick remembers going up to the house as a child in the springtime, when the whole pathway was bordered with daffodils.

He says the couple was very happy and had a cosy existence. Mr Hoban was an ex-British soldier. Mrs Hoban grew black-currants, gooseberries and apples, and Dominick still remembers the taste of the gooseberry jam she made, which she would have throughout the winter and into the following spring.

People used to go up to the Hobans in the early spring to borrow a hen to hatch their eggs. The farm was small, and they supplemented their income by selling eggs. In those days a basket of eggs would buy the week's groceries.

The couple's cottage was also used as a gambling house – people from around the area would come in the evenings to play the card game 25. Mr Hoban would play the piccolo for entertainment. They had no children, and when they died in 1963, the house was left empty and sadly is now in ruins.

Sandstone Bridge

The land on both sides now starts to rise above the level of the track, and in the distance an old overhead bridge of reddish stone comes into view. The road over this bridge forms part of the Oghillies Burrishoole Loop Walk, the beginning of which you passed at Lough Fadda.

Some distance after this, you come to another wooden bench, so placed as to afford a splendid view of Croagh Patrick and the surrounding countryside. A little further along, a plantation consisting partially of lodgepole pines springs up to the north, looking like a fine big stand of Christmas trees.

Soon after this you reach a bollard in the middle of the path, and the surface of the path turns from grit to tarmacadam. In late summer, the north verge of the road here is bright with thick magenta clusters of Rosebay Willowherb shot through with the blazing orange fireworks of Montbresia.

Eventually you come to Gate 34. A road running north-south intersects the track. Across the road Gate 35 marks the entrance to the next section of track, with a big barn to the left or south. The track here reverts to grit and continues straight ahead, with level pasturelands full of sheep stretching out to both sides.

Humpbacked Bridge

Within a short space, there are two more gates, 36 and 37, and soon after these, Gate 38. The trees gradually

Sneezewort

Centaury

Rosebay Willowherb and Montbresia

Humpbacked bridge

thicken a bit, and ahead looms an old humpbacked stone bridge, with a bench just in front of it, surrounded by drifts of golden Ragweed.

Knockbreaga

On the other side of the bridge is a small stream, issuing from Carheenbrack Lough to the north. Farther along, a lane-way transects the track, ending at a large farm up on a hill to the north. From here you can see the traffic on the main road, and just ahead is Gate 39. This area is called Knockbreaga.

From Gate 39, you can see Gate 40 a short distance ahead. Between the two gates, to the north, are a couple of old stone dwellings. The smaller one possibly dates from the 1800s, and the other, a hipped-roof house, was probably built in the late 1800s or early 1900s. Possibly the family who lived here moved from the smaller house into the larger one.

Townlands

Townlands are an important aspect of Irish social, economic and political history. They are the smallest units of administrative land division, based on pre-Norman Gaelic systems. Many have retained their original Irish names, often becoming corrupted by English usage, whilst some are of more recent origin.

The Irish names can have interesting meanings, such as Knockbreaga, which in Irish is Cnoc Bréige, meaning 'false or treacherous hill'. Fear Bréige means 'a false man or something shaped like a man', which was sometimes applied to a Liagan or standing-stone. Thus, this hill may have once had such a stone on its summit.

Townlands vary in size, from less than an acre up to 7,012 acres, though typically they are between 200 and 400 acres. Their size is linked to the agricultural quality of the land, with larger townlands having poorer quality land.

Old ruins at Knockbreaga

Just beyond Gate 40 is a bench, and here you cross through open farmland, with no fencing to separate you from the sheep. You pass through two more gates in fairly rapid succession – Gates 41 and 42 – and then come to a small latched gate (Gate 43), with a hand-written sign requesting you to keep the gate closed at all times in the interest of stock and safety.

Here you enter onto a small road, running north-south, and on the other side is Gate 44, beside a small cottage. Through the gate, the banks rise up to shoulder-height on either side, with a sprinkling of wildflowers, including the delicate pink Ragged Robin, the lavender-blue pincushions of Devil's Bit Scabious and spikes of Purple Loosestrife.

Farm to north of Greenway at Knockbreaga

Purple Loosestrife

Rockfleet Castle

Due south of Knockbreaga is a large, sheltered bay called Rockfleet Bay. On its innermost reaches stands Granuaile's last stronghold, Rockfleet Castle, also known as Carraigahowley, from the Irish Carraig an Chabhlaigh, meaning 'rock of the fleet'.

Granuaile was born on Clare Island around 1530, in a castle that still stands guard over the small harbour there. As a girl she was determined to go to sea with her father, but as a female, she was not allowed to sail, and it is said that she shaved off her hair in an attempt to disguise herself as a boy, thus earning her the nickname Gráinne Mhaol, or 'Bald Grace'.

She became the chieftain of the seafaring O'Malley clan and Queen of Umaill, an ancient territory all along Clew Bay, between the Baronies of Murrisk and Burrishoole. The O'Malleys frequently traded with Spain and Scotland and taxed all boats that fished in their waters. They also engaged in piracy.

Granuaile was a skilled and intrepid mariner and became captain of a fleet of galleys. She commanded 200 men who helped her defend her trading interests and fight against the English military, which attempted to curb her power.

In 1546, she married the heir to the O'Flaherty title, with whom she had three children. The O'Flahertys ruled what is now Connemara. After her husband was killed in battle, she married Risteárd an Iarainn Bourke, or 'Iron Richard', a powerful man who owned Rockfleet Castle. They had one child together.

In the latter part of the 16th century the English intensified their encroachment upon Irish territories. In 1593, when two of her sons and her half-brother were captured by the English governor of Connacht, Granuaile traveled to London to petition Queen Elizabeth I for their release. She was well-educated and conversed with the Queen in Latin, as neither woman spoke the other's language. The queen took a liking to her and granted her request, provided she cease to rebel against English forces.

Granuaile spent her latter years at Rockfleet Castle, and it is said that her boat, which was moored just below the castle, was tied to her bed at night. The castle itself has been extensively restored and is well worth a look.

Ragged Robin

Gradually the banks level out and stretch away into moorland, with the Glennamong Mountains rising to the north and rough pastureland to the south.

Owengarve River

Some distance ahead, you come to a straight timber bridge with blue railings crossing over the Owengarve River. On the other side of the bridge is an information board with a simplified map of the area. There is also a bench here and just beyond that, Gate 45.

The Greenway runs straight as a ruler from here, with low verges, affording frequent glimpses of the Owengarve River winding through the marshy land to the south.

Soon you come to a small path branching off from the Greenway to the south, which leads to a small

Fishing

The Owengarve River used to be well-known for its good fishing. In the early 1900s plans were made to erect a wooden platform here to let guests from the Mulranny hotel off to fish, as the Midland & Great Western Railway had bought the fishing rights for the river. Whether or not the platform was ever built, people were dropped off here upon request.

Owengarve River

Footbridge over the Owengarve River

weathered timber bridge across the river. This was constructed about 40 years ago from girders left over from the railway track. The surrounding land was bought from CIÉ by a farmer who used the bridge to take sheep up and down.

Old Ford

The vegetation along here is quite rough, composed mostly of prickly Thistles, Rushes, Gorse and bush-like plants of Burdock with their spiny brown burrs.

Ruined Cottage

Eventually you come to Gate 46. Just through this, on the south side, is an old farm gate with a track leading down to the river. Here an old ford of large stepping stones crosses to an overgrown boreen on the opposite side. It's a charming spot and well worth a look.

From here the track undulates gently through open marsh and moorland, with rolling, verdant hills stretching off to the south of the river. A bench on the south side of the path invites the weary traveller to take a rest while contemplating the meandering river and the many hues of green in the valley, which contrast with the blue wash of distant mountains.

Glenthomas River with old stones of original bridge visible

Glenthomas River

A little farther on is Gate 47, which opens onto a passage across the Glenthomas River. While this doesn't appear to be a bridge, just beyond the verges of the path you can see the old stone structure of the original bridge underneath.

Old Ford

The boreen on the other side of the ford connects up to the main road and is still used to move sheep across the stepping stones to the commonage above the old railway track.

According to local farmer and County Councillor Michael Holmes, in bygone days this was a busy passageway, with sheep and cattle being brought across the stepping stones and up to the commonage on the other side of the railway track.

Farmers would use the ford in the mornings and evenings to go up and milk their cows. Turf was cut in the bog above and transported back across the stones by donkeys with creels.

Because of the constant stream of traffic across the tracks here, a level crossing was installed. It was manned by a Mr McLoughlin, who was given a standard railway cottage nearby. Its ruins stand beside the Greenway, and the inhabitants must have once enjoyed a fine view of the river below.

Borehole in cutting

The track continues on much the same, with the river soon fading from sight. After a while you come to Gate 48, and from here the banks on both sides rise steeply. This is obviously an old shallow railway cutting, and occasionally you can see a rock with a bore hole where dynamite was used.

Newfield Inn

Eventually the shoulders along the side of the pathway drop again, and straight ahead you come to a sign advertising Nevin's Newfield Inn, in Newfield or Tiernaur, urging you to turn left for food and refreshments. They even offer a courtesy car to come and collect you!

Ahead the track is paved and you reach a pair of bollards, followed by Gate 49. Through the gate you come to a crossroads: the road towards Nevin's heads south, while the other

Newfield Inn

This is one of the oldest inns in Mayo, dating back to the 1700s. The original owner, Dinny Sweeney, was closely related to Father Manus Sweeney, who was found guilty of treason for his involvement in the rebellion of 1798 and was hanged in Newport.

In the same century the McLaughlin family built a residence nearby called Newfield House. During the 1800s the local landlord, James Hunter, moved in, and in 1869 he was shot dead. The wake was held at Newfield Inn, during which an attempt was made to ascertain the identity of his murderer.

According to the Burrishoole Loop Walks brochure, produced by the Newport Tourist Office, "During the construction of the Westport to Achill railway line between 1894 and 1900, Newfield Inn was a central rendezvous point for the workers. It also included a food store servicing the area stretching from Mulranny to Newport."

side heads north through a farm gate with a style next to it, and turns into a gravel track. This heads up into peat bog in the foothills of the Nephin Beg Mountain Range and joins up with the Greenway again farther along.

The Greenway continues straight on through another couple of bollards, and the surface turns to grit again, with scrubby hills to the south and bog stretching away endlessly towards the mountains in the north. If you look back towards the road to Nevin's in the east, you can see an old ruined cottage on the hillside, and there are others nearby.

Bog road near Tiernaur

Bog Roads

During WWII roads were created up into the peat bogs nearby in order to gain access to turf. This was cut and shipped up on the train to Dublin, as coal was scarce at the time.

Active Farmland

The track continues straight for a while until suddenly it narrows considerably and twists to the north and immediately west again. Here the fencing on the south side comes tight up to the track, and there is a prominent sign proclaiming that you are entering onto active farmland. The fencing continues for quite a stretch, and just before the end, you can see a ruined cottage through a gate to the south.

Rosturk

The pathway widens out again, and a gravel track runs off from the south side of it. A little farther along, a paved road runs up to the south edge of the path from the main road. In the distance to the south you can see the old whitewashed Rosturk Post Office along the main road, just across from where this road comes out.

The surface of the path changes to tarmacadam here. Just a short way along, views of the sea unfurl, with Croagh Patrick looming across Clew Bay. Then for a short stretch the south verge of the Greenway becomes crowded with small

trees, mainly Willow and Rowan, but then opens up again, with bog extending to both sides and splendid views of Clare Island in the distance.

Along this section of the Greenway wildflowers are rather scarce, consisting mainly of Kidney Vetch, Tormentil and Knapweed, and there is a fragrant patch of deep pink Japanese Rose on the south verge.

Shortly after this you reach three bollards, and just

Rosturk Castle

Just south of the Post Office, Rosturk Strand rims a small peninsula, upon which stands Rosturk Castle. It is surmised that this was the site of another O'Malley stronghold, possibly under the control of 'Diabhal An Chorráin', or 'Devil of the Sickle', who may have been Grainuaile's son-in-law.

The old tower house, which may have been one of four held by the O'Malley clan, was built onto in the mid- and late 1800s. It now comprises the north-western corner of the present-day castle, which was constructed in the Victorian Gothic style. Its ownership has changed hands a few times, and it is now rented out as holiday accommodation.

View of Clew Bay from open bogland

beyond them the surface is brand-new and smooth as it charges on between high banks. At the end of this section you reach Gate 50.

Steep Bogland

On the other side of the gate the track takes a right-angled bend to the north, and immediately you come to Gate 51, which is a small latched gate. To the west you can see where the original track continued straight on across a ridge of bog and into a thick stand of tall trees surrounding a house.

Stepping through the small latched gate is like striding out onto the top of the world. The path climbs up through rocky, open bogland, which is commonage. It offers stunning views of the surrounding countryside and Clew Bay. The surface of the track is very rough, and it is the steepest part so far. There are signs all along it warning cyclists heading downhill to be careful and to dismount.

At the very top the path meets a small road. The left side runs in a southwesterly direction, down to the main road by the Bunnahowna road bridge. To the right it veers away northeast into the mountains, where it turns into a rough gravel track. This meets up with the wartime bog-road from the crossroads near Tiernaur.

Bogland

Blanket Bog

The area to the north of the trail is covered in Atlantic Blanket Bog, one of three types of bog in Ireland: Atlantic Blanket Bog, Mountain Blanket Bog and Raised Bog.

The first is found along coastal regions from sea level to an altitude of around 200m (656ft). It has a grassy appearance, as the predominating vegetation is Purple Moor Grass (*Molinia caerulea*) and Black Bog Rush (*Schoenus nigricans*). It tends to be fairly wet, with pools, flushes and swallow holes.

Mountain Blanket Bog is found on relatively flat mountain slopes above 200m (656ft). Heathers, Crowberry and Bilberry proliferate here. It also contains lakes and flushes. The main characterising feature of blanket bog is that it occurs in an area where evaporation cannot keep pace with high rainfall, and it is generally fairly shallow, from 2m (6.5ft) to 7m (23ft) deep.

The formation of blanket bog began after the last glaciation 10,000 years ago, when shallow lakes and damp hollows began to fill in with partially rotting vegetation. About 4,000 years ago the climate here underwent a change and became much wetter. By then the island was thickly forested with Scots Pine and deciduous trees.

Neolithic man had arrived and begun to clear the forest for agriculture. The clearing of trees left the soil vulnerable to erosion, and along with the wetter conditions, minerals such as iron were leached from the surface layers of soil and deposited lower down, forming an impenetrable layer called a pan. Because the water could not seep through this layer, the ground became water-logged, and as more nutrients were washed away with the rain, the soil became very acidic.

Only a few plants could survive on this acidic ground, and due to lack of oxygen, their debris did not fully decompose. As a result, a layer of peat began to build up. This is a dense, compacted brownish-black substance composed of dead mosses, grasses and heathers which are only partially broken down and have built up on top of each other over thousands of years.

Gradually this engulfed the trees, and as their seedlings could not survive the acidic soil, the forests began to die out. Tree stumps are still preserved in the bog to this day and are known as bog oak or bog pine. Pollen grains from thousands of years ago are also preserved in the peat, telling the story of what plants grew here in the past.

Raised Bog

Raised bogs, on the other hand, occur mainly in the midlands.

They were formed when shallow lakes began to fill with plant material, which, because of the anaerobic conditions, did not completely decompose. In time this material began to form a firm layer of peat which filled the hollow. Sedges grew on top of this, forming a fen, which thickened so that the roots of plants could not reach the calcium-rich groundwater.

Subsequently, their only source of water was rain-water, which is mineral-poor. Only species such as mosses that could survive this habitat moved in, and the fen became a raised bog, consisting of a soft, living carpet of floating vegetation with a thick layer of rotted, compressed moss, or peat, beneath, which can be up to 12m (39ft) deep.

Bogs are important habitats for a rich biodiversity of species, including rare plants, invertebrates, insects and birds.

They are also a vital reservoir of water and an important carbon sink, which helps to control greenhouse gases leading to global warming.

Peat bogs absorb more carbon per hectare per year than tropical rainforests. There are not many left in the world, and Ireland plays a significant role, possessing 8% of the bogs that remain on the planet. They are the most valuable area of bog habitat in Europe.

At this junction you are directed to turn left and a short way down, right again, towards the west. At this stage, the Greenway has not yet merged again with the original railway track. That is yet to come.

Bunnahowna Railway Bridge

The original track to the south is covered with tall pine trees. The path snakes along beside it, finally arriving at a truly spectacular sight: a massive sandstone railway bridge towering above a foaming river.

Considering that this stately bridge was constructed well before the days of modern machinery, it is a testament to the immensely hard work and impeccable engineering of our forebears.

Before the bridge, you bear left, or south, and cross through Gate 52. This is a small latched gate, bearing the sign, "Keep gate 'CLOSED' In the Interest of stock and safety AT ALL TIMES. 'Thank You'." This section is fenced in with wooden slats, and the pine trees covering the original track lap up against it. Just below them you can make out a large

Commonage

Much of the Greenway crosses through commonage, which is communally-owned land on which two or more farmers share grazing rights. It is not physically divided, but the number of shares tenants have is related to the size of their farms. The system has its origins in Ireland's ancient Brehon laws.

During the early part of the 19th century it became known as the Rundale system, under which the land directly surrounding farmhouses was used primarily for cultivation while the common higher ground was used for livestock grazing. During the Land Reforms between 1869 and 1909, when tenants were incentivised to buy their farms from their landlords, these upland tracts of land were considered unprofitable and therefore unsuitable for division. Thus commonage grazing rights continue to this day.

Old Railway Bridge over the Bunnahowna River

water tower. The fencing crooks west, and partially blocking the original track onto the bridge is a peculiar sandstone hut, like a crenellated sentry-box.

From the top of the bridge it is dizzying to look down at the Bunnahowna River rushing below the single tall arch. Springing out of the riverbank to the south side of the bridge is a tall stand of graceful Scots Pines.

As you continue on, the view of Clare Island is breathtaking. Wildflowers are abundant along here. There are patches of St. John's Wort, Tutsan, Burdock and the delicate pale pink fronds of Bog Pimpernel.

Bog Pimpernel (*Anagallis tenella*)

The Park

As you approach Gate 53, a curious sight unfolds. Monumental sandstone walls, taller than a man, extend along both sides of the track, running uphill to the north and spanning the brow of the slope.

This is known locally as The Park. These colossal walls, while tumbled down in some sections, range as far as the eye can see, reminiscent of the Great Wall of China, albeit on a much smaller scale!

The verges here are stony, and only a few wildflowers venture out, including the exquisite Heath Spotted Orchid, the tiny yellow blossoms of Tormentil and the starry golden tufts of Bog Asphodel, like small sparklers.

Sentry Box

This little hut was built sometime during the last century after the railway closed down.

Danny Callaghan, who lives nearby, claims it was built by Richard George Browne, an auctioneer in Westport, as a little hut in which people could sit and read or write and contemplate the wonders of nature, as was fashionable at the time. Browne's brother was the Bishop of Galway. Browne owned a railway cottage at a level crossing just to the east, by the part of the track that is now covered in trees. He subsequently sold the cottage to the Martins, who sold it on to the Foxes.

Others say the hut was built by the Foxes to shelter in when they were out walking There is another theory that it was actually used as a sort of sentry box to keep an eye on the river and protect the landowner's fishing rights from poachers.

The Bunnahowna Bridge is also known as Washpool Bridge. Local women would bring their clothes for washing to the river pools below, long before the bridge was built.

The Park

Some stories have it that the Stoneys, local landlords in the 19th century, had these mighty walls constructed to contain deer. Others state that they were built as a folly, pointing out that the roughly six hectares they contain are steep and not ideal for grazing. Yet others say that the landlord had them built simply to create employment for local people during difficult financial times.

When the railway came through, one of the walls had to be rebuilt. A noticeable feature of the walls is the stones regularly protruding from them. It is thought that they were used either for tying the walls together or as scaffolding in their construction.

According to local knowledge, there were originally three sections to The Park, and one was planted with trees in the mid-1800s. By the time the train came through, the plantation was fairly mature.

However, one day some sparks from the burning coal of a passing locomotive ignited the dry sedge along the tracks near the plantation, and the flames spread to the trees. The blaze ravaged the plantation, reducing most of the trees to cinders. Only a few Scots Pines remain near the Bunnahowna Bridge.

Heath Spotted Orchid

Once through Gate 54, the walls extend for a short distance, and then give way to sheep fencing. Bog rises on both sides, eclipsing the sea. Patches of snowy-white Bog Cotton stand out against the olive Rushes.

Spa Well

Eventually you come to a beautiful sandstone well just on the north verge, its smooth round basin full of crystal-clear water. This was called the 'Spa Well'. Trains would stop here and collect water to take up to Dublin to sell for its healing properties.

Soon Corraun Hill, beyond Mulranny, looms closer. Wildflowers are again more abundant along the edges, and the sea becomes visible again. Conveniently, there is a bench on which to rest and admire all this beauty.

Just beyond is Gate 55, and on the other side, an information board with a detailed map. However, the road which joins the track at this point from the south is not shown on it. The surface now changes to tarmacadam, continuing on through Gate 56.

Spa Well

Murrevagh River

From this gate you come to a bridge over the stony Murrevagh River. Its railings are cleverly fashioned from old railway sleepers and fence posts.

You may see Dippers (Gabha Dubh in Irish) here. The size of a Blackbird and dark brown with a white 'bib', they will dive and actually walk along the river bed searching for insect larvae.

Bog Plants

Bog Cotton is a type of sedge and was once used as a stuffing for pillows and mattresses. It was also used to produce candlewicks and dressings for wounds.

Rushes were used for thatching and were also dipped in melted tallow, twisted together and mounted on a slit stick, which was stuck into a sod of turf, to serve as a light.

If you look closely you may even see Sundew or Lesser Butterwort, both carnivorous plants that have adapted to the nutrient-poor bog environment by digesting insects for nourishment. Sundew has distinctive reddish leaves with pin-shaped tentacles, whilst the Butterwort has a beautiful violet flower. Both trap the insects in their sticky leaves.

Mulranny-bound!

Soon you can see the sparkling harbour and village of Mulranny ahead. When the tide is out, the vast expanse of sand-flats glisten like a smooth shield of silver in the light. What a thrill this view must have been to the holiday makers that neared Mulranny by train so many years ago!

Mulranny

Eventually you reach a barn on the right, and up ahead you can see a cluster of signs and buildings. The original track continued straight on to the railway station, but this has all been built up in recent years.

Instead, you follow the road left and downhill towards the main road – there's a sign here urging cyclists to dismount, as it is quite steep. Before reaching the bottom a sign directs you to a road on your right.

This takes you up behind the village, and down to another road. Ahead is a signpost directing you to join this road, which comes up from below, curving around a tight bend and continuing on more or less straight ahead from the road you have just come out of.

Up ahead you skirt close by black gates at the entrance to modern apartments. You go around behind these buildings, close by another small building to your right. At the far

corner of this building you will see bicycle and pedestrian symbols on the pavement.

Keep going, along the whitewashed stone wall to your left, and soon you will see the red brick water tower of Mulranny Station ahead of you. The Greenway comes out at the brick ruins of the railway station, just behind the Mulranny Park Hotel.

Water tower at Mulranny Railway Station

If you have worked up an appetite, you may enjoy a meal at the hotel, which is another member of the Gourmet Greenway Trail. They are also famous for their fresh-baked breads, which you can purchase to take with you on a picnic. They also host regular exhibitions of the Greenway Artists. Their website is: mulrannyparkhotel.ie.

Another local member of the Trail is Murrevagh Honey, which is a small hobby apiary owned by James McDermott and Derek Norton. The honey, which has a very light colour and a delicate flavour, is harvested by hand using a spinner. To arrange a viewing of the hives, you can email jmcdermott47@gmail.com.

Achill Sound
Achill
START FINISH
74
73
70
66
65
61
Tonregee
Owenduff
452
Lough Gall
Cartron River
Lough Namachan
Cuillaloughaun
Glennanean Riv.
R319
524
541
Corraun Hill

Mulranny to Achill Sound

In a nutshell

The distance from **Mulranny to Achill Sound** is 13km (8 miles). The estimated cycling time is 1–1½ hours, while walking should take 4–4½ hours.

The track from Mulranny starts off through woodland, with tantalising glimpses of Bellacragher Bay to the northeast. Eventually the woods thin out, and for the most part the Greenway rolls on across open farmland, heath and bog, with striking views of the bay to the east and north and mountains in all directions. It passes by a small lake down by the sea, and crosses several small streams.

Much of this section passes through Special Areas of Conservation, under which rare and important species and habitats are protected. These are considered valuable from both a European and Irish perspective.

By Dánlann Yawl Gallery the Greenway merges with the main road for about 700m (766 yards) and then swings off-road again, continuing across heath, rough farmland and blanket bog, some of it worked by turf-cutters. The gallery is well worth a visit, as is the basket-weaver farther along the way.

About a kilometre and a half short of Achill Sound, the Greenway again merges with the main road, which brings you to the end of the line near the old railway station.

Mulranny's Setting

The Irish for Mulranny is An Mhala Raithní, which means 'slope of bracken', Spanning a panoramic section along the north side of Clew Bay, it commands fine views across the water to the majestic peak of Croagh Patrick on the south side of the bay. Extensive white sandy beaches grace its shores, while rugged mountains loom at its back.

A distinctive feature of the village is the causeway that was built across Trawoughter Bay in the late 1800s, from the historic hotel out to what is now a blue flag beach. This crosses two important habitats: the salt marshes that have formed

behind the beach, and Rossmurrevagh machair.

The salt marshes inhabit the area between the sandflats and the shoreline and are characterised by a complex drainage pattern of small brackish channels winding between swards of vegetation cropped by grazing sheep. They support a wealth of flora, including Sea Thrift, which turns the entire salt marsh to a dainty pink froth in May.

Many birds come to feed and rest here, among them the Grey Plover, Oystercatcher, Widgeon, Curlew, Godwit, Dunlin, Sandpiper, Snipe, Lapwing, and various Gulls and Terns. Brent Geese also overwinter here. Salt marshes occur in many parts of Ireland, but one of this size is rare.

The machair is located between the salt marsh and the sandflats, surrounding a small shelter along the causeway.

Salt Marsh

Rossmurrevagh Machair

It is a sandy grassland, composed of siliceous sand from glacial sediment and calcareous sand derived from seashells.

Marram and Lyme grass, as well as wildflowers such as Daisies, Common Bird's-foot Trefoil, Lady's Bedstraw and White Clover, grow here and are also cropped by grazing sheep. Globally, machair is found only along the northwest coasts of Ireland and Scotland, and it is one of the rarest wildlife habitats in Europe.

The Mulranny to Achill section of the Greenway starts at the red-brick remains of the once-elegant Mulranny Railway Station behind Mulranny Park Hotel.

The ruined station is owned by the hotel and is a listed building. There are plans afoot to refurbish it for use as an interpretation centre.

The old red-brick water tower on the opposite side of the track was once used to replenish the tanks on board that provided steam to power the old locomotives. It was supplied with water from streams in the hills behind the station.

Brick ruins of Mulranny Railway Station

Out from Mulranny

Starting from the dilapidated station the Greenway runs past several modern residential buildings to the south, with wild-flower verges on both sides, some smothered in large patches of the pernicious and vigorously invasive Japanese Knotweed. It then plunges into mature woodland.

The steep banks along here are evidence of a cutting that was blasted out of the rocks. Above the stand of Spruce trees to the north towers Claggan Mountain, 383m (1,257ft) tall at its highest point. The woodland through here is a mixture of predominantly native trees such as Oak, Ash, Larch, Holly, Scots Pine and Rowan. It is interspersed with Rhododendron, which is another invasive species, introduced into Ireland from the Iberian Peninsula and Asia in the 18th century.

You may spot Treecreepers (Snag in Irish) along here, which are small grey-brown birds, similar in size to the Blue Tit. They scale the trunks of trees searching the bark for insects with their slightly curved bill.

Soon you approach the first gate in this section – Gate 56. Beyond it is an information board with an excellent map. An

Mature woodland with Claggan Mountain beyond

access gate from the N59 also enters here. Beside the information board is a bench cleverly constructed of sculpted bronze old-fashioned suitcases which look so realistic that they readily summon up visions of train travel a century and more ago. These were created by Tim Morris, as mentioned previously. There is also a plaque with a photograph of Mulranny Railway Station in its heyday, as well as a handy bicycle stand constructed from fence posts.

Gate 57 (on right) and bridge across the N59 to Ballycroy

Bridge Across the N59

After this you reach Gate 57, which opens onto a straight wooden-railed bridge crossing above the N59 to Ballycroy.

Shortly after the bridge across the N59, you will see a pole to the left with a solar panel on top. This is a counter to provide Mayo County Council with data on how many people use the Greenway. There are three of them along the route.

On the other side of the path there is a sign for the Lookout Hill Loop Walk, pointing towards a railing that angles

Ballycroy National Park

About 10km (6 miles) up this road is the Ballycroy National Park, one of Ireland's six national parks. It contains 11,000 hectares of Atlantic Blanket Bog and mountainous terrain, which support a variety of habitats and species.

Within this vast unspoilt wilderness of upland grassland, alpine heath, lakes and river catchments, species such as Greenland White-fronted Geese, Golden Plovers, Red Grouse and Otters can be found.

Admission to the visitor's centre is free, and it and the tea room are open from March to the end of October. There are a number of stunning walks through the park, as well as guided tours.

Old Irish Goat

All along this section keep an eye out for wild goats. Mulranny is extremely fortunate to have a population of Old Irish Goats. This species is quite distinct from other types of goats. It is quite small and stocky, with short legs, small ears, a delicate face and a very thick, long coat. The males have impressive beards and sideburns, an extravagant quiff and extremely long horns.

Their undercoat has a thick layer of cashmere, hearkening back to harsher, colder weather in prehistoric times. The overcoat is vari-coloured – mottled or streaked with white, grey and reddish-brown. They are what is known as a landrace breed, shaped by and for the landscape.

Domesticated in prehistoric times, they were used for their hair, hides, skins, horns, flesh and fat. They are extremely well-adapted to our native habitat, and they were the only breed of goat that Ireland had until Victorian times, when British varieties were imported from England.

Since then, these and Swiss breeds have interbred with the Old Irish Goat, and there is no telling how many pure native species still exist. There have been no surveys carried out to date. Of all the wild goats in the country, perhaps 10-15% are of the Old Irish type. They are extremely rare and facing imminent extinction as a distinct species.

There are about 20 Old Irish Goats left in Mulranny, and you may spot them between October and May along the Greenway. They may be mixed in with a herd of other feral goats, numbering close to 100.

Mulranny Environmental Group has plans to start a breeding programme for the critically endangered goats. To support their efforts, contact: carolan.sean1@gmail.com. For more information about the Old Irish Goat, you can go to: www.oldirishgoatsociety.com.

Old Irish Goat, © John Joyce, by permission

sharply down the steep bank. This is a walk with truly breath-taking views, leading into the slopes of Claggan Mountain, which rise up just north of the Greenway. It then takes you down across the sparkling bay in front of the Mulranny Park Hotel. The hill section of the walk can be rather rugged in places, and depending upon your preferred pace, the entire walk takes anywhere from 2 to 4 hours.

Bellacragher Bay

Along here magnificent views of Bellacragher Bay open up to the north, and there is a series of thoughtfully-placed benches on which to relax and enjoy them. Gazing out at the bay, you may be lucky enough to glimpse visiting Dolphins (Deilf in Irish) or Seals (Rón Beag). You might also spot birds such

Irish Heath

Irish Heath, © Sue Callaghan, by permission

Another rare species found on Claggan Mountain and also, to a lesser extent, around Lough Furnace, is the Irish Heath (*Erica erigena*), also known as Mediterranean Heath. Radio carbon dating places its introduction to the area at around 1431.

Like St. Dabeoc's Heath, it was probably introduced to the area by pilgrims and also through trade with countries in which it occurs, such as Portugal and Spain, where it was used as packing material for bottles of wine.

It looks somewhat similar to Bell Heather, except the flowers are a bit smaller and much paler. It blooms between March and May and sometimes in winter; whereas Bell Heather flowers from May to September.

Generally Irish Heath flourishes on wetter terrain than Heather. Within this country it only grows in isolated pockets in the counties of Mayo and Galway.

View over Bellacragher Bay to the north

as the Peregrine Falcon, Greenland White-fronted Goose, Golden Plover and even the Golden Eagle.

At some of the benches along here there are plaques with old photographs from the Lawrence Collection of the railway line when it was still in use. There are also additional bronze antique suitcases, some of which appear to have been dropped from the traveller's hands in sheer amazement at the spectacular view that greeted them upon alighting from the train! A little farther along you will see a small steel sculpture of a bull on top of a pillar.

Bull sculpture by Ronan Halpin

Sculpture Trail

Entitled 'Precipice', this sculpture of a bull was created by Ronan Halpin and is part of the temporary Greenway Sculpture Trail, devised by the Greenway Artists

Notable Birds

The Peregrine Falcon (Fabhcún Gorm in Irish) is a large, powerful bird with a shortish tail, long, pointed wings and a short, hooked bill.

The upper parts are blue-grey, and the underparts are pale and finely barred. It has a black hood and prominent 'mustache'.

It preys mainly on smaller birds, taken in the air or on the ground or water. Its hunting technique is to dive-bomb its prey with wings held close to the body, using its legs at the last moment to inflict a fatal blow. It is the fastest bird on earth, reaching speeds of up to 240kph (149mph).

Peregrine Falcon, © Anne Burgess, CC BY-SA 2.0

From October to April flocks of rare Greenland White-fronted Geese (Gé Bhánéadanach) may be spotted flying overhead towards Ballycroy. These are medium-sized grey geese with a dark-barred belly, orange legs and a pink or orange bill with a broad white base. They breed in Greenland in the summer and are one of Europe's rarest geese.

Golden Plovers (Fheadóg Bhuí) may be heard calling. These plump, medium-sized birds, spangled with black and gold markings, have a variety of sounds, including a "pu-pee-oo" which is repeated in display flights. They breed on blanket bog and heathery moors, and are found in large flocks in the winter-time.

Golden Eagles (Iolar Fíréan) may also be spotted in this area. These magnificent birds, which have a wingspan of up to 2.3m (7.5ft), were exterminated in Ireland in the early 1900s. They were re-introduced to Donegal from Scotland as part of a breeding programme and have gradually worked their way down the west coast. They may be seen soaring silently overhead, with spread, up-curved wing-tips and a square tail, hunting for prey such as small mammals and large birds.

Golden Plover, © Ferran Pestaña, CC BY-SA 2.0

Initiative in conjunction with the Custom House Studios and supported by Mayo County Council and Mayo Naturally.

There are a number of other pieces located at different points along the Greenway and also down at Westport Quay. The Greenway Artists are a dynamic group, and no doubt other works of art will play a part in the constantly changing Greenway experience.

The track continues through woodland with frequent glimpses of the bay and eventually arrives at a large green sign proclaiming that you are entering active farmland. Some distance ahead you will come to a gate with a sign saying "PRIVATE FARM KEEP OUT."

Here the track bends sharply right and then left, passing between sheep fencing with green fields on either side. The original railway line continued straight ahead from the sign on the gate, passing through a present-day farmyard. On the other side of the farmyard it merges again with the Greenway, which passes through Gate 58, normally open.

It runs between a combination of wooden and wire sheep-fencing and veers north between the sea and the N59, which runs close along the west (or left) side of the track. Just along here the active farmland comes to an end, although if you are

Black-faced Mountain Sheep

The type of sheep along here is the Black-faced Mountain sheep, which is smaller and hardier than its lowland cousins.

It is able to withstand the harsher conditions of the west coast and can survive on plants such as Heather that other livestock cannot. Both male and female have horns and black or black- and-white faces and legs. They have long coarse wool which protects them from rain and biting winds.

Bellacragher Bay with mussel rafts in the distance

cycling it is still wise to look out for sheep along the track, as they wander freely throughout this section.

Cuillaloughan River

Gradually the woodland begins to thin out. You pass a sheep pen on the right, and just ahead is a small wooden-railed bridge across the narrow Cuillaloughan River, which flows down from Cuillaloughan Hill to the west, part of Corraun Hill. After this, a big green barn perches above the track to the left, and a short distance ahead on the same side is another

Sea Trout Farm

Across the bay is a fish farm called Curraun Blue. Operated by Tom and Tom Dougherty, a father and son team, it is the only producer of organic sea-farmed Trout (*Oncorhynchus mykiss*) in the country.

Only natural or organic ingredients are used in the Trouts' diet, and the farm adheres to a policy of very low stocking densities. Curraun Blue is a member of the Gourmet Greenway Trail. Their email is curraunblue@eircom.net.

Rough jetty in small cove on Bellacragher Bay

small sheep pen. Here the landscape opens up, with boggy land to either side and unimpeded views of the bay, dotted with fish farm nets and mussel rafts.

Glennanean River

Next you come to wooden railings on both sides. While it doesn't look much like a bridge, this crosses over the Glennanean River, which also has part of its source in the Cuil-laloughan Hills and partly in a small lake to the northwest, called Lough Namachan.

Up ahead are Gates 59 and 60, both of which are staggered. Between them a rough track scrambles steeply uphill towards the main road to the west (or left), and to the east (or right) is a small lane which runs along a snug cove where a small group of boats bob at their moorings. The landscape directly to the north side of the cove is a working peat bog, and ricks of turf can be seen drying on the banks in the summer.

Lough Gall

From Gate 60 the track runs between sloping banks covered with grasses and heathers. On the east bank there is even a very unusual small patch of white Ling, a type of

Heather with very small, usually lavender flowers.

Shortly thereafter the track emerges into open countryside, heading straight as an arrow through fairly flat boggy ground, with views of the sea to the east and rugged mountains in all directions. Soon the sparkling waters of Lough Gall come into view close to the east side of the track. This is part of the Lough Gall Bog SAC. Although it is a protected area, some turf-cutting for domestic use is allowed. One can imagine taking a refreshing dip in the lake after a few strenuous hours of cutting in the bog!

Turf ricked up and spread out to dry near Lough Gall

Ahead, to the west side, is a small abandoned quarry, possibly used to obtain stone for the railway track beds. A short distance from this you come to Gates 61 and 62, also staggered. Between them runs a lane from the main road down along the north shore of Lough Gall and then parallel to the track for quite a stretch, ending at a farm in the distance.

Lough Gall

Cartron River

Humpbacked bridge over Cartron River

The track continues much the same, with the jutting mountain to the west near Owenduff soaring to 452m (1,483ft). This is called Tonregee, meaning 'backside to the wind'. Between this mountain and the Corraun Hills lies a forested valley full of small lakes and rivers. It is from this valley that the meandering Cartron River originates, and presently you come to a humpbacked wooden bridge with blue metal railings, which crosses over it.

After a while you arrive at Gate 63, which is not so much a gate as a cattle grid. Just to the right is a steep incline, and down below you can see the Cartron River curving around to run close beside the track.

Active Farmland

Beside the gate is a Trail Notice advising you that you are entering active farmland. The track narrows and carries on for a considerable distance between sheep fencing on both sides, bordered by farmland.

Off to the east, between the track and the sea, you can see the green fields and red barn of the farm at the end of the lane that runs between Gates 61 and 62.

Eventually the section of active farmland comes to an end, you pass through Gate 64, which is also half gate and half cattle grid, and the track widens again. A few trees grow along the edges, and wildflowers are more abundant here.

The track passes close behind a house and some sheds on the left, while on the right is an old sandstone ruin. Just after this, wooden fencing stretches along both sides, leading you to the mouth of the Cartron River, where it empties out into the sea.

Cartron Estuary

Along here are plaques displaying interesting tidbits of history relating to migrants from Achill and to the old Westport

Merlin, © U.S. Fish & Wildlife Service CC BY 2.0

Ravens and Merlins

Keep an eye out for Ravens (Fiach Dubh in Irish) along here, which breed on Corraun Hill. They are pure black and our largest songbird, 60-67cm (23.5–26.5 inches). They exhibit acrobatic displays, often flying upside-down.

Merlins (Meirliún) also inhabit the forested area around Corraun Hill. These are birds of prey (raptors) and the smallest falcon, 27–32cm (10–13 inches). They are fast and nimble fliers, often flying low in pursuit of other birds. In particular they prey on the vulnerable Meadow Pipit, which nests on the ground in bogland. They have pointed wings and a square tail. The male is blue-grey above, while the female is brown. Both are heavily streaked below with bars across the underwing.

Raven, © Atli Harðarson, CC BY 2.0

Plaque displaying local history, overlooking the Cartron estuary

to Achill Railway – these are well worth reading.

Just beyond this is an information board, where you can see that you have only 6km to go to Achill Sound.

Although clearly the original train track continued straight on through the undergrowth here, the path takes a sharp bend to the west (or left) and climbs up to the main road. Just before you come onto the road there are signboards stating "CAUTION: Primary road for 700 m. You will re-enter back onto Greenway in 700 m."

Greenway emerging onto main road by the Dánlann Yawl Art Gallery & Coffeeshop

Dánlann Yawl Art Gallery

At the top are signs for the charming Dánlann Yawl Art Gallery and Coffee Shop, in case you are feeling in need of a bit of refreshment and cultural enrichment.

Whether you have ducked inside the Dánlann Gallery for a bit of culture or are coming straight off the Greenway, take great care emerging onto the main road here. The speed limit is 80kph, and for cyclists there is

Dánlann Yawl Art Gallery

A distinctive Achill Yawl with a bright red sail is painted on the gable end of the cottage-like gallery. Its owner, Seosamh (Joseph) Ó Dálaigh, welcomes visitors with a kindly smile.

Originally from Westport, he has occupied this scenic spot for 28 years, teaching and painting. He is passionate about his artwork, which fills the walls of his small gallery.

He exhibits one or two other artists and has an array of local crafts, such as hand-knitted scarves, framed tapestries, pottery, cards and bookmarks. He also sells a modest range of art supplies.

The tearoom, with its stunning views across the bay, is just that: tea, coffee, home-made scones, jam and cake, nothing more. He prefers to keep things simple, and while he welcomes cyclists and passers-by and will accommodate larger groups who contact him ahead of time, he does not cater for throngs of people.

He is set up primarily as an art school and gallery, and is geared more towards small groups of people who want to attend his art classes. These, he says, deal with every aspect of art and operate on not just a practical but also on a spiritual level, helping students to find their 'inner colour'.

The gallery and tea-room are open from April to October. The website for the gallery is: www.achillpainting.com.

Greenway Artists

At this point it is worth mentioning the Greenway Artists Initiative, an extensive group of local established visual artists, including painters, photographers and sculptors who have joined together for exhibitions. They also run classes, talks and workshops in the area. The initiative provides support to all artists within the county, and they hold monthly exhibitions in Mulranny Park Hotel.

no verge whatsoever. In places there are very narrow grassy verges that a pedestrian can avail of. Fortunately the road is fairly straight, so the visibility is good. The railway line originally went close along the road, and there are plans to widen the road here, keeping the Greenway on the seaward side.

Re-start of the off-road Greenway along from the Yawl Gallery

Tonregee

700m farther along you will see a Greenway sign on your right. This takes you a very short way down a small lane onto the continuation of the Greenway proper.

The landscape along here is mostly open boggy land with a few evergreen trees and houses, with splendid views of Blacksod Bay to the north. A short distance ahead you approach Gate 65, which is staggered, close to a distinctive flat-roofed house with crenellations.

From here the path carries on for quite a way between

Tonregee Siding and Viaduct Across Bellacragher Bay

Originally the Midland and Great Western Railway had plans to erect a two-storey train station near this region of Tonregee. The station was never built, but upon request, trains would stop here to collect or deposit mail and passengers. A siding was also constructed to service a nearby fishing pier. However, this was not extensively used, and after some years it was dismantled.

Another proposal was put forward in 1893 to add a track branching north from the railway line between the areas of Owenduff and Tonregee. It was to cross Bellacragher Bay to Ballycroy via a long viaduct and carry on up to Belmullet. As this line would have been very expensive to construct and would have passed through large stretches of uninhabited land, the plans never came to fruition.

Slievemore in the distance on Achill Island, across Blacksod Bay

chain-link fencing. Presently the fencing on the right comes to an end and the path curves sharply to the left, joining a small lane for a short distance.

This takes you almost up to the main road again and then turns right, off the lane and back onto a grit pathway. A short way along here a magnificent view opens up of Slievemore in the distance on Achill Island, across the bay.

To the south you can see Tonregee National School nestled at the foot of the looming hill of Tonregee. The school just turned 100 years old in 2011.

Soon you reach Gate 66, a staggered gate. On the other side of this is a small lane going from the main road down to the sea. The track continues straight across the lane close to a house called Railway Cottage and crosses a small bridge over the Sruthán Buí, or 'Yellow Stream'.

The path winds a bit after this and then straightens out, continuing on through boggy land studded with Heather and Rhododendron bushes.

After a while you come to Gate 67, again staggered, and this takes you out onto a small paved lane which merges with the Greenway. The laneway runs between sheep-fencing and a stand of pine trees, passing by a house with a riot

Small abandoned cottage with Gunnera by the front door

of flowers planted by its gate. Soon it reaches another lane leading from the main road down to the sea.

Directly across the lane is a tiny abandoned cottage with blocked-up windows, dwarfed by a huge clump of Gunnera, which reaches to the top of the doorway.

Blacksod Bay

The Greenway resumes across the lane to the right of the small cottage. Here, by a stand of pine trees, you enter Gate 68, again staggered. The track climbs very gently, and at the top is a bike rack and bench with a fine view of Blacksod Bay and the two closest islands: uninhabited Annagh Island to the east

Rhododendron

These bushes are invasive and love acid soil. They are a big problem in many parts of Ireland, as they crowd out native species, and concerted efforts have been made to eradicate them. Other parts of the immediate area have become overrun with them, and it is possible that they will take over this area too.

Gunnera

This is a South American species that was introduced to Ireland in 1939 as an ornamental plant. Its foliage is amongst the largest in the world – one leaf can extend up to 2m (6.5ft).

It possesses glands that can fix nitrogen, enabling the plant to thrive in very poor soils. It reproduces both by seed and by vegetative propagation, and has spread like wildfire in large parts of Achill and Connemara.

As it shades out other native plants, it has become a pest in these areas, and ongoing efforts to control it have been underway for some time.

Corraun Hill emerging from behind Tonregee Hill

and to the west Inishbiggle (Inis Bigil in Irish), which means 'Island of Fasting'.

From here the track descends slightly and runs parallel to a small road, which eventually merges with the track. Shortly thereafter it intersects another lane leading from the main road down to the sea.

Inishbiggle

While it lies only a stone's throw from Achill Island, the waters in between the two islands, called the Bull's Mouth, have among the fiercest currents in Europe, cutting the small island's 22 inhabitants off from the mainland for long periods in the wintertime. The islanders subsist mainly on cattle- and sheep-farming, fishing and winkle-picking.

Basket-Weaver

A sign here points towards the bay, indicating a "Coffee Shop and Basket Weaving Workshop Ahead."

On the other side of the lane down to the basket-weaver, you pass through Gate 69, which is staggered. From here the track runs straight for a long way and crosses an old stone bridge above a small stream. Corraun Hill, violet-blue in the distance, begins to slide back into view from behind Tonregee Hill.

Up ahead another lane from the main road merges with the track. Farther along you come to another small quarry on the north side. After this you pass through Gate 70, which is actually two open black gates.

Here a rough track crosses the Greenway, heading from the main road to the sea. Just after this you cross a cattle grid, and the path narrows considerably, running for a stretch between sheep-fencing. The landscape is very open here, with flat bogland to either side. Soon you begin to see signs of turf-cutting, with long dark trenches carved out of the peat bog.

The track sweeps on across flat stretches of bogland and eventually arrives at Gate 71, which crosses a cattle grid. On the other side of this, a laneway from the main road cuts across and plunges down to a ruined cottage by a little rocky cove. Nearby is a traditional whitewashed cottage with a stand of pine trees. In the next field over is another ruined cottage, with sheep grazing beyond it.

An alternative route back to the main road from Gate 72

From here the track is paved, until you reach Gate 72, a double gate, which is normally open. Here another lane winds across the bog and crosses the track, down to the sea. Although the Greenway continues straight on and joins up with one final small road, the top of the laneway by Gate 72 merges with the same final road farther up towards the main thoroughfare.

Kathleen McNea in her tea-room/shop with her hand-made baskets

Basket-Weaver

Just a few paces down the road, this little shop is well worth a visit. Kathleen McNea of Cáit's Ciseáns has a warm welcome for everyone and is delighted to see so many people using the Greenway.

She learned the craft of basket-weaving from her father, Michael Kilbane, who made baskets for the entire Achill community. In those days everyone used baskets for turf, spuds, eggs, and as side-creels, or 'pardóg', for donkeys.

When her father died in the early '80s, she decided to continue his tradition. Kathleen still makes fine turf and spud baskets, but has adapted as well to modern times: you can pick up a rustic hand-made basket for your bicycle for a very reasonable price.

She also runs a small tea-room, which is open in the summer months. She sells her wares and teaches basket-making all year round and, for a small fee, will give you a demonstration of basket-weaving on the spot.

She works from home and her small shop is behind her house – just follow the signs up the driveway. Kathleen's website is: www.achillbaskets.com.

Turf-cutting

Although nowadays most turf is cut by machine, it used to be extracted by hand using a sleán or slane, a traditional tool resembling a narrow spade with a wing on it. With a single thrust, the sod is cut on two sides, and with a twist of the slane, the sod is detached from the bog and swung up onto the bank.

In the summertime the sods are gathered up into small stacks called ricks, which are laid out in patches to air. After the turf has dried it is collected, and big piles of it can be seen heaped up beside the track.

It is still used as a main source of fuel for heating by many people in the area, though in parts of the country certain bogs have been protected and turf-cutting is restricted. There has been a great deal of controversy over this issue, with those having turbary rights (the right to cut turf for domestic use) in these areas clashing with the government, which is under pressure from the European Commission to protect our dwindling peatland habitats.

In order to avoid being heavily fined by the Court of Justice of the European Union over our failure to protect our peatlands, the government has designated 53 raised bogs as Special Areas of Conservation, where peat-cutting is heavily restricted.

To remain on the Greenway, you continue straight on. Soon you come to Gate 73, which has a cattle grid, and just through the gate are an information board, bike rack and bench with a lovely view of Blacksod Bay and Slievemore.

Achill end of Greenway proper

End of Greenway Along the Railway Track

From here it is only a short distance to the end of the Greenway following the original railway track. It comes out onto a small road at Gate 74, which has a cattle grid at the side of a small house. Across the lane here is a sign directing you to your left (or south) towards Acaill (Achill), and you follow this up to the main road.

Beside the directional sign here is a rusty gate, and through this you can see a raised area that was clearly the continuation of the old railway line. It is now completely overgrown with Rhododendrons.

At the top of the lane is a signpost, with one sign for the Greenway which points back down the road you just came up, and the other pointing west towards Achill. You turn right (or to the west) here and proceed about 1½km (almost a mile) along the road to Achill Sound.

Be extremely cautious along this road, as it can be quite busy. There is no verge for cyclists, while for pedestrians there are some grassy shoulders. There are plans to either widen the road here to accommodate the Greenway or to continue the Greenway off-road along the original railway track

Information board and photographic plaque before the bridge across Achill Sound

all the way to Achill Sound.

After some distance you can make out the the white arched bridge across Achill Sound up ahead. On your left, near the Achill Island Hotel (Ostan Oileán Acla in Irish), you will see a plaque with an old photograph of Achill Sound Railway Station and an information board. Most of Achill Island is a Gaeltacht area.

Old station house, now a hostel

What is left of the old railway station is just across the road from the hotel. It is now closed to the public, except for the old station house, which is currently a hostel.

Greenway sign along main road from Achill Sound

If you are starting off on the Greenway from the Achill side, you go east along the main road (the R319) from Achill Sound for roughly 1½km (nearly a mile) until you see the signpost for the Greenway on your left. Again, be careful with the busy traffic along here. Follow this side road down to the sign for the Greenway and Westport, and pick up the trail there.

Gourmet Trail

Two final Gourmet Greenway members are located on Achill Island: Achill Island Turbot and Keem Bay Fish Products.

Achill Island Turbot is Ireland's only Turbot farm. Turbot is a large flat-fish with both eyes on the left side. For more information about their business and tours, you can go to their website at: www.achillislandturbot.ie.

Keem Bay Fish Products produce smoked organic Salmon, Mackerel and kippers in their own smokehouse. The owner is also the proprietor of the excellent seafood restaurant The Chalet in Keel. Their email is keembay@gmail.com.

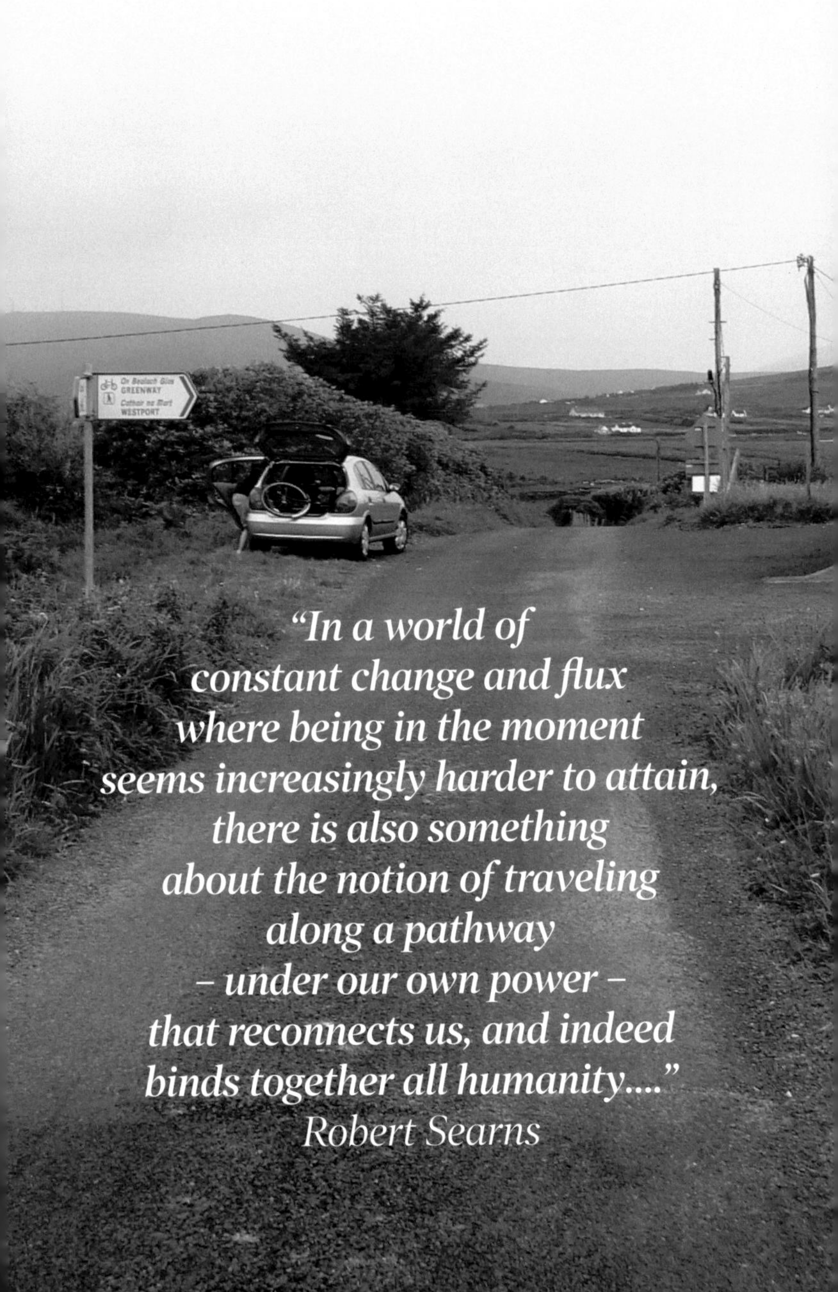
GREENWAY
WESTPORT
"In a world of
constant change and flux
where being in the moment
seems increasingly harder to attain,
there is also something
about the notion of traveling
along a pathway
– under our own power –
that reconnects us, and indeed
binds together all humanity...."
Robert Searns

Wildflowers Along the Greenway

This section showcases a variety of wildflowers commonly found along the Greenway, including information to help identify them, along with a few details of interest.

I also have provided a brief summary of some of the traditional uses of each plant. I would like to emphasise that, in the instance of medicinal usage, I am only reporting historic practice, and *I am not in any way recommending the herbal remedies described.*

In all cases I have provided the common name in English, the scientific name and the Irish name. Where the Irish names have a different meaning from the English, I have added the English translation in inverted commas.

It is my hope that this may enhance your enjoyment and appreciation of the rich plant life that nature has to offer along the Greenway.

Please don't pick the wildflowers – leave them for others to enjoy.

Angelica, Wild
Angelica sylvestris
Ainglice

Wild Angelica can grow up to 6 feet tall, with umbrella-like heads of tiny green-white flowers and purplish stalks. It has inflated purplish sheaths at the base of its stalks, which encapsulate the developing flower-heads. It is found in damp grassy places and woodland from July to September. Traditionally, it was used to treat a variety of ailments, from rheumatism and gout to indigestion and flatulence. It has been used for flavouring liqueurs, and its stems are still candied to decorate cakes. Great care must be taken not to mistake it for Hemlock (*Conium maculatum*) or Hemlock Water Dropwort (*Oenanthe crocata*), both of which closely resemble Wild Angelica and are highly poisonous. Hemlock has purple-spotted stems and a strong, fetid smell.

Bindweed (Hedge)
Calystegia sepium
Ialus Fáil

A creeping plant with white trumpet-shaped flowers, found from June to September in woodland, waste ground and fens. It binds itself around other vegetation, thus the name. It has been used as a strong purgative and also to reduce fevers and inflammation of mucous membranes. It is considered a pest by farmers and gardeners, as it can be difficult to eradicate: one tiny piece left in the ground can regenerate.

Bog Asphodel

Narthecium ossifragum

Sciollam na Móna

Spikes of small starry yellow flowers, rather resembling sparklers, arising from a base of short sword-shaped leaves. The stalks are a bright orange and are found in boggy places from July to August. The plant was also called "bone-breaker," as it was believed that livestock grazing on it suffered from brittle bones. In fact, this was due to the calcium-poor vegetation growing in the same habitat. Bog Asphodel was once used as a substitute for saffron and also as a yellow hair-dye.

Bramble

Rubus fruticosus

Dris

A rambling thorny creeper, best known for its sweet blackberries, which are not only delicious to eat, but have been considered medicinal as well, blackberry jam having been used as a curative for throat problems. In fact, most parts of the bramble were regarded as useful; the leaves have been used for curing diarrhea as well as cuts and burns, while the roots were carved into pipes and provided an orange or dark green fabric dye. The shoots were used for baskets and thatching. It flowers from May to November, while the berries ripen in the early autumn. Found in woodland, scrub, grassland, hedges and waste ground.

Burdock, Common
Arctium vulgare
Copóg Thuathail

A tall, stocky plant with large downy leaves and distinctive purple-brown marble-sized burrs which cling onto hair, fur and clothing. Its egg-shaped purple flowers bloom from July to September, and it is found on waste ground, sand dunes and open land. The root contains an ingredient that purportedly lowers blood sugar and thus has been used to treat diabetes. Among many other curative properties, it was also reputed to be useful in relieving eczema and other skin complaints.

Buttercup, Creeping
Ranunculus repens
Fearbán Reatha

This unmistakable shiny buttery-yellow flower will be familiar to everyone, growing abundantly in meadows and along roadside verges. The plant is quite toxic, containing an acrid juice that can blister skin, and it is avoided by cattle. However, cooking or drying it removes the poison, and it was eaten during the Great Famine. As a counter-irritant, it has been used to treat rheumatism and muscular pains. It blooms from May to September.

Celandine, Lesser

Ranunculus ficaria
Grán arcáin

These sunny rayed flowers with their glossy heart-shaped leaves lift the spirits in early spring. One of the first blossoms to appear at the end of winter, they spread their bright message of cheer along the woodland floors. The word Celandine originates from the Latin chelidonia, meaning 'swallow', as the flowers were said to appear when the swallows did. The plant was also called 'pilewort', as its knobbly roots were held to resemble piles, and was therefore used to treat haemorrhoids.

Centaury

Centaurium erythraea
Céad Dulleach
'hundred leafed'

The many-branched stalks of this plant bear deep pink star-shaped flowers that only open when the sun shines. It grows in grassy places from June to September. Extremely bitter, Centaury was used for indigestion and as a tonic to purify the blood. In addition it was used to treat wounds, liver and kidney problems, and muscular rheumatism. A lotion was made to soften facial skin and clear it of blemishes, freckles and age spots.

Cinquefoil, Marsh

Potentilla pallustris
Cnó Léana
'water-meadow nut'

This unusual star-shaped reddish-brown flower grows in marshes, bogs and acid fens, blooming from May to July. A decoction of the root was used for stomach cramps. The flowers were used to produce a red dye, and tannin was obtained from the roots.

Devil's Bit Scabious

Sucissa pratensis
Scaibeas Greim Diabhail

This beautiful purple-blue flower with rounded pin-cushion-like heads grows in damp grassy places. Its roots were considered powerful medicine, and it was used as a remedy for many ailments, from plague to fever to wounds. The word is derived from scabies which it was used to treat. (*Scabere* is the Latin for scratch.) Its root ends abruptly, and it was thought that the devil had bitten it off because he was angry that it possessed such formidable healing properties. It was especially used for skin complaints, such as dandruff, blemishes and sores. Notably, it is the primary larval food of the critically endangered Marsh Fritillary butterfly. It blooms from June to October.

Eyebright, Common

Euphrasia officinalis
Glanrosc

This is a very low-growing flower with tiny, almost orchid-like blossoms, white with a violet or bluish tinge and sometimes a yellow spot. It grows in grassy places and heaths, blooming from June to October. It is actually a parasite, attaching itself to the roots and stems of grasses. As its name implies, it was used for all eye complaints. A more recent finding is that it may be useful in treating hay fever and heavy colds if applied to the nose and throat every few hours.

Figwort, Common

Scrophularia nodosa
Fothram/Donnlus
'brown plant'

This dramatically tall plant has only tiny waxy reddish-brown flowers. It grows in shady, wooded places and blooms from June to September. It was regarded as the queen of herbs, just as the Foxglove was the king. It was considered a powerful fairy herb and was used to cure a variety of ailments, such as bronchitis, sprains and burns. It was also used as a remedy for piles, known as "figs," thus the name figwort.

Foxglove

Digitalis purpurea
Lus Mór
'big plant'

Like the Figwort, Foxglove is a very tall plant and, surprisingly enough, it also of the Figwort family. Its distinctive tubular bell-shaped flowers are a bright pink-purple with white-speckled inner lips. It grows on open ground and woodland, heaths, mountains and scrub, and blooms from June to October. The spots on its flowers show up vividly in ultraviolet light, enticing bees to crawl into them. It contains the powerful heart-regulating drug digitalis and can be quite dangerous. Nonetheless it was widely used as a cure for sore throats, colds, fevers and heart complaints. Some people believed that if they added a little bit of it to their daily beverage, they would be granted long life.

Goldenrod

Solidago virgaurea
Slat Óir

A short to medium-sized plant with branched spikes of small short-rayed bright yellow flowers, blooming from June to September. It is found in scrub, rocky places, grassland and heaths. Goldenrod was used as a cure for cystitis; it was also used for stomach and kidney complaints as well as rheumatism, arthritis and thrush. A salve was made of the flowers for application to bruises and wounds. The plant yields mustard, yellow, orange and brown dyes. It was considered an all-round useful plant.

Bell Heather

Erica cinerea
Fraoch Cloigíneach

A short to medium-sized shrubby plant with spikes of small bell-shaped violet-red flowers that blanket vast areas of bogs, heaths and open woodlands. Flowers from July to September. Heather's springy branches were used for brooms, bedding and fuel. It was also considered a valuable medicinal plant and used for a wide variety of ailments such as insomnia, asthma, cystitis, colds and coughs, rheumatism, arthritis and gout.

Herb Robert

Geranium robertianum
Ruithéal Rí
'king's herb'

This small five-petaled deep pinkish flower graces many a hedgerow and shady place from April to November. This little plant contains germanium, which is purported to have the capacity to make oxygen available to the body, and thus may play an important role in boosting the immune system. There is even some evidence that it may help to fight cancer. It was commonly used for kidney complaints and sore throats and to staunch bleeding. Farmers also utilised it to cure red-water fever in livestock.

Honeysuckle
Lonicera periclymenum
Féithleann

Pictured opposite, the fragrant clusters of Honeysuckle are the essence of summer. The tubular creamy yellow- to rose-coloured flowers grace our hedgerows and woods from June to October. It was also known as Woodbine, for its ability to bind tightly around small trees and bushes, choking off their growth. Because of this it was regarded as a symbol of strength and relentless power. The blossoms are full of a sweet nectar, and they were eaten to cure a sore tooth. They were also used as a gargle for mouth inflammations such as thrush and sore throat. Reputed to be a natural antibiotic, Honeysuckle was valued for reducing fevers and purging toxins.

Iris, Yellow Flag
Iris psuedacorus
Feileastram

This tall plant with distinctive flashy yellow flowers and sword-shaped leaves brightens ditches, marshy land and damp places throughout the summer months. It spreads by means of rhizomes, the underground segments of the stem, which have nodes that send out shoots and roots. The leaves were commonly dried and used for bedding, fodder and even thatching. They also produce a pale yellow or bright green dye, while a bright yellow dye is extracted from the flowers, and the root yields a black or brown dye. The tannins in the root have also been used for making ink. For toothache a sliver of the rhizome was held against the afflicted tooth to bring relief. The juice of the roots was also used as a remedy for coughs and colds.

Ivy

Edera helix
Eidhneán

Ivy is a familiar sight, climbing up trees, walls and hedgerows. An evergreen, its clusters of tiny yellow-green flowers bloom from September to November and have a strong cloyingly sweet smell. The flowers are followed by small black berries, favoured by many birds, which also find year-round shelter in its leaves. Ivy was held to be a powerful expectorant and was used to treat congestion and bronchitis. It was used as a cure for skin conditions, such as eczema, and also to treat aches and pains, arthritis, boils and corns.

Knapweed, Common

Centaurea nigra

Minscoth

A medium-sized plant with violet-red rayed thistle-like flowers, scaled rather than spiny, blooming from June to September in grassy places. It was used as a tonic, as well as a cure for jaundice, liver problems, loss of appetite, sore throat and bleeding of the nose and gums.

Lady's Bedstraw

Galium verum

Bolach Cnis, Boladh Cnis, Rú Mhuire

'cattle skin', 'skin odour', 'Our Lady's Rue'

A low, rambling perennial with small dark green leaves and clusters of tiny yellow four-petaled star-shaped flowers, very fragrant. It blooms from June to September in dry, grassy places. A highly versatile plant, it was traditionally used to stuff pillows and mattresses, not only for its lovely scent, but also to aid sleep and repel fleas (thus the name bedstraw).

Legend has it that this comprised the bedding of the manger in Bethlehem, hence the association with the Irish name for our Our Lady, Muire. It was used in cheese-making to curdle milk and to give it a bright yellow colour. The stems and flowers were used as a yellow hair dye, while the roots produced a red colour that was sometimes used to dye wool and other fabrics. Medicinally it was employed for skin complaints, hysteria, vertigo and epilepsy. It is also a preferred food plant for the caterpillars of the Broad-Bordered Bee Hawk-Moth, which has transparent wings and mimics a bee's appearance.

Lady's Smock

Cardamine pratense
Biolar Muire
'Mary's cress'

This is also known as 'cuckoo flower', as it blooms around the time the first cuckoo is heard in April. A medium-sized plant with pale pink four-petaled flowers, it is a member of the mustard family and grows in meadows and damp places. It is high in vitamin C and minerals and was used as a general springtime tonic. It was also believed to help nervous conditions such as epilepsy, hysteria and even St. Vitus' dance. In addition, it has been be used for menstrual disorders and abdominal cramps. Externally applied, it is said to promote blood-flow to the skin's surface and was used for skin irritations, rheumatism and arthritis.

Loosestrife, Purple

Lythrum salicaria
Créachtach

A tall plant, with striking spikes of bright purple-red flowers, usually growing in wet areas in large colonies of vivid colour from June to August. It was used as a cure for diarrhoea, dysentery and tonsillitis. It was also employed as a wash for sore eyes and was considered by some to be superior to Eyebright in this respect. The stems were chewed to treat bleeding gums. Purple Loosestrife also has the property of being able to break down environmental pollutants into inert compounds.

© M. J. Richardson, CC BY-SA 2.0

Lords-and-Ladies
Arum maculatum
Cluas Chaoin
'smooth ear'

This distinctive plant has large arrow-shaped leaves. Its flower consists of a pale pinkish lily-like sheath containing a purple-brown rod and appears in April and May. In the autumn it has a spike of bright red berries, which are poisonous to humans. It is also called Cuckoo Pint or Arum Lily and grows in woods and on shady banks. The small potato-like root was considered nutritious when baked and was once given to invalids under the name Portland Sago. In Elizabethan times, the elaborate ruffs worn by aristocrats were stiffened with a starch made from the roots. Mixed with milk it was used as a remedy for freckles, blemishes and wrinkles. An ointment for ringworm was also made from the root.

© Paul Henderson, CC BY-SA-3.0

Marsh Marigold

Caltha palustris
Lus Buí Bealtaine
'yellow plant of May'

The bright yellow flowers of Marsh Marigold were picked to adorn houses on May eve in order to protect them from evil forces and fairies. A member of the buttercup family, it has glossy kidney-shaped leaves and blooms in marshy places from March to June. Although all parts of the plant are toxic and irritating to the skin, it was used as a traditional cure for fits, warts and anaemia. Occasionally the leaves and roots were boiled and eaten as a vegetable, and the buds cooked, pickled and used like capers.

Meadowsweet

Spiraea ulmaria
Airgead luachra
'silver rushes'

The tall fluffy white heads of fragrant Meadowsweet can be found in marshes, ditches and wet meadows throughout the summer. The common name comes from 'mead-sweetener', as it was used to flavour mead, beer and wine. It was also mixed with rushes and scattered on floors to keep the house smelling pleasant. In addition, it was used to scrub out milk vessels and to manufacture a black dye. It contains salicylate, a main component of original aspirin, and was used to treat aches, colds, influenza and fever.

Mint, Water

Mentha aquatica

Mismin Mionsach

Water mint has hairy toothed leaves and rounded spikes of tiny lilac-pink flowers that bloom from July to September. It grows in ditches and damp places. When the leaves are crushed, they have a wonderful minty aroma, and the leaves were chewed to freshen the mouth. Traditionally it was strewn on floors to impart a fresh scent to the room. It also helped to repel fleas and moths from bedding and clothing and was placed in stores of corn to keep mice away. It was used to alleviate nettle stings, to cure coughs, colds and indigestion; and a thimbleful of the juice was poured into the ears to treat deafness.

Nettle, Common

Urtica dioica

Neantóg

A medium to tall plant with toothed, heart-shaped leaves and drooping catkins The stems and leaves are covered with fine, stinging hairs that contain the same formic acid as stinging ants. It is found throughout the summer months in woods and on waste ground. The Nettle had many uses. Its fibres were employed to manufacture a strong, fine, silky cloth. It also produced a yellowish green dye. The fresh leaves were boiled and eaten like spinach or in soups and used as a springtime tonic. It was used to treat rheumatism and arthritis and is still made into a hair rinse to alleviate dandruff and to add shine.

Pennywort/Navelwort

Umbilicus rupestris
Cornán Caisil

A small plant with a 'navel' in the centre of round fleshy leaves. It grows on walls and rocky banks, and its spikes of yellowish-white flowers can be seen throughout the summer. It was particularly valued for treating kidney stones and other kidney problems. It was also used for skin conditions, chilblains, corns and sore eyes. Its young leaves were eaten either raw or cooked.

Plantain, Ribwort

Plantago lanceolata
Slánlus
'health plant'

A short plant with elongated ribbed leaves and blackish knobby flowers with a ruff of pale yellow anthers. It is plentiful in grassy land and waste ground from April to October. It was used since ancient times to staunch bleeding, and the juice was drunk to alleviate coughs. It has been used to treat a wide variety of ailments, such as diarrhoea, peptic ulcers, irritable bowel syndrome, cystitis, bronchitis, asthma and hay fever. A gold or brown dye was obtained from the plant.

Primrose

Primula vulgaris
Sabhaircin

Everyone is familiar with this cheerful light-yellow flower bursting out on grassy banks and woodland floors in the early spring. Occasionally it can be found blooming in the autumn and winter as well. Primrose was used to treat insomnia, toothache, burns, nervous headache, gout and hysteria. It was also considered an expectorant and was used to clear the lungs of catarrh. The flowers were sometimes pickled.

Ragged Robin

Lychnis flos-cuculi
Lus Síoda
'silk plant'

This pretty knee-high plant has distinctive bright pink flowers, with deeply lobed petals which make them look somewhat ragged. It grows in ditches and damp meadows from May to August. It was used to treat jaundice, toothache, stomach ache, headache and strained muscles. The root contains saponins, which were used as a soap substitute for washing hair and clothing.

Ragwort, Common

Senecio jacobaea
Buachalán Buí
'yellow ragwort'

A medium to tall plant with dense flat-topped heads of small bright yellow daisy-like flowers, blooming from June to November. It is found on nearly every roadside verge and grassy field. Although it is an important food source for many invertebrates, in Ireland it is considered a noxious weed, and landowners are required to control its growth. Whilst it is poisonous to livestock, it was used externally to treat cuts, sores, burns, ulcers, colds and sore joints. It was also used to make brooms and was stored with oats to repel mice.

Redshank/Persicaria

Polyganum maculosa
Glúineach dhearg

This medium-sized plant has spikes of small dense pink or white flowers sprawling over disturbed or bare ground from June to October. It was said to have grown at the base of the cross, and the dark spots in the centre of its narrow pointed leaves were believed to be the drops of Christ's blood. Oddly enough, the plant was used to staunch bleeding. It was also used to treat stomach pains and as a foot and leg soak for rheumatism.

St. John's Wort, Perforate

Hypericum perforatum
Lus na Maighdine Muire
'plant of the Virgin Mary'

This medium-sized plant has small star-shaped golden flowers with tiny black dots on the petals. The leaves have small oil glands which look like minute windows when held up to the light. It grows on grassy verges and banks, blooming from July to September. It was well-known for treating depression and was also used for healing cuts and wounds, sore eyes, diarrhoea, dysentery and bladder problems. Infused in oil, it was a remedy for rheumatism, back pain and sciatica.

Self-heal

Prunella vulgaris
Duán Ceannchosach

A low creeping plant with dense spikes of tiny tubular purple flowers in bloom from June to November, Self-heal is found on grassy, damp and bare ground. Among its many virtues, it is said to possess antiseptic and antibacterial properties and was valued as a panacea. It was used especially for treating wounds, heart problems, fevers and tuberculosis. There has also been some research into its therapeutic possibilities in treating cancer, AIDS and diabetes. The leaves and small flower-heads were regarded as edible and were used in soups, salads and stews.

Silverweed

Potentilla anserina
Brosclán

A low-growing creeping plant with toothed pinnate silvery-green leaves and small five-petalled flowers, Silverweed grows by roadsides, waste ground and damp grassy places throughout the summer. Before the advent of the potato, it was much prized for its tuberous roots, which were boiled or roasted or dried and ground into a powder for making bread. It was also used to treat diarrhoea, bleeding piles, heart problems, internal bleeding, mouth ulcers, loose teeth and running sores.

Sneezewort

Achillea ptarmica
Lus Corráin
'scythe plant'

A medium-sized plant with small saw-toothed leaves and modest white daisy-like flowers with greenish-cream centres, Sneezewort blooms from July to September along damp verges, moist grassy places and acid soil. While it is poisonous to livestock, it has been used as a refreshing tea, and the leaves were chewed to soothe toothache. It was also employed as an insect repellent. The leaves were once dried and ground and used as a sneezing powder.

Speedwell, Germander

Veronica chamaedrys
Anuallach
'arrogant'

A short plant with broad, bluntly-toothed leaves and small very bright blue flowers with a white eye, Speedwell blooms in woods, grassy places and hedgerows from April to June. It was used for coughs, to purify the blood, for kidney complaints, skin diseases and itching. In fact, it was considered a panacea for many diseases, including smallpox, measles and cancer.

Tormentil

Potentilla erecta
Néalfartach
'dozing'

Tormentil is a member of the Rose family. It is a low, creeping plant with small four-petalled bright yellow flowers and is found on moors and grassy places from May to September. Traditionally, the roots were boiled in milk and the liquid given to calves and young children against colic. The same concoction was also used to cure diarrhoea. In addition, it was mixed with St. John's Wort to alleviate insomnia. A decoction of the herb was used to cure foot rot in sheep. Tormentil has a high tannin content, which made it useful in treating serious burns and for tanning leather. Tannin from tree bark was originally used for tanning, but during the 18th century, when trees became scarce in Ireland, the Royal Dublin Society introduced a scheme to encourage tanners to use Tormentil roots for their trade.

Tutsan

Hypericum androsamemum
Meas Torc Allta
'fruit of the wild boar'

The sunny five-petaled golden flowers of Tutsan are quite distinctive with their frothy stamens and large paired leaves that turn chartreuse in late summer and purplish in autumn, accompanied by shiny purple-black berries. They prefer shady areas, along embankments and woods, and flower from June to August. The name Tutsan comes from the French *toute-saine*, which means 'all healthy'. It is related to St. John's Wort and was held to share some of its anti-depressant qualities, although its main virtue lay in dressing cuts, wounds and burns. Additionally it has been used to treat sciatica and gout. The antiseptic properties of the leaves have also been used to preserve cheese.

Valerian, Common

Valeriana officinalis
Caorthann Curraigh

The tall flat pale-pink strongly scented heads of Valerian add a lift of colour and aroma to ditches and damp grasslands throughout the summer. Best known as a sedative and sleep aid, it was also used to treat epilepsy, irritable bowel syndrome, headaches, neck aches and asthma.

Wild Strawberry

Fragaria vesca
Sú Talún Fiáin
'wild juice of the earth'

The long runners of the Wild Strawberry, with their toothed trefoil leaves and small white five-petalled flowers, can be found in the spring on shady banks and at the edge of woodlands. The berries follow in the summer and, while very small, are quite tasty and sweet. They also have properties which purportedly helped to destroy kidney and gall stones, and they were used to ease the distress of gastroenteritis. The root was used to treat dysentery, diarrhoea, cystitis and bronchitis, while the leaves were recommended for tuberculosis, gout and joint pains.

Willow-herb, Rosebay

Epilobium angustifolium
Lus na Tine
'fire plant'

The imposing spikes of bright magenta Rosebay Willow-herb can be found growing on open woods, heaths and waste ground throughout the summer. It is one of the first plants to grow back after a fire, thus the Irish name 'fire plant'. It has been used to treat diarrhoea, dysentery, irritable bowel syndrome and abdominal cramps. Cordage can be obtained from fibres in its tough stems, and the downy seeds were used as stuffing material. When cooked, the young shoots were said to make a tasty asparagus substitute.

Wood Avens/ Herb Bennett

Geum urbanum
Macall Coille

The long stems of Wood Avens with their pinnate leaves and small star-shaped yellow flowers can be found in shady places, especially on fertile soils, from May to September. The flowers are followed by finely-hooked burrs that cling onto passersby. Its roots, which have a clove-like scent, were used in medieval times to repel insects and to flavour ale, as well as to ward off evil spirits. Externally it was used to treat vaginal discharges and skin afflictions, while administered internally it was said to alleviate stomach, liver and intestinal disorders.

Yarrow

Achillea millefolium
Athair Thalún
'father of the land'

This short to medium-sized plant has narrow, deeply toothed leaves and large flat heads of tiny white flowers which bloom from June to November. It grows in grassy places and along verges. Yarrow was highly valued for staunching bleeding in gums, cuts and wounds, as well as internal bleeding. It was said to induce perspiration and was used to battle coughs, colds and fevers. The fresh leaf applied to an aching tooth was reputed to soothe the pain. The flowers yielded a green or yellow dye.

The Flora Protection Order

When the last Ice Age ended around 10,000 years ago, Ireland was connected to Europe by land bridges, across which animals, plants and trees migrated. Sea levels rose as the ice melted, and the land bridges vanished beneath the water, causing Ireland to become isolated from the rest of Europe. Consequently, Ireland's biodiversity is relatively low compared to that of Europe.

Of the approximately 6,500 plants we have in Ireland, 89 are protected under the Flora Protection Order of 1999. It is illegal to cut, pick, uproot, damage or remove parts of these plants. A complete list of these plants can be obtained at: http://www.irishstatutebook.ie/1999/en/si/0094.html.

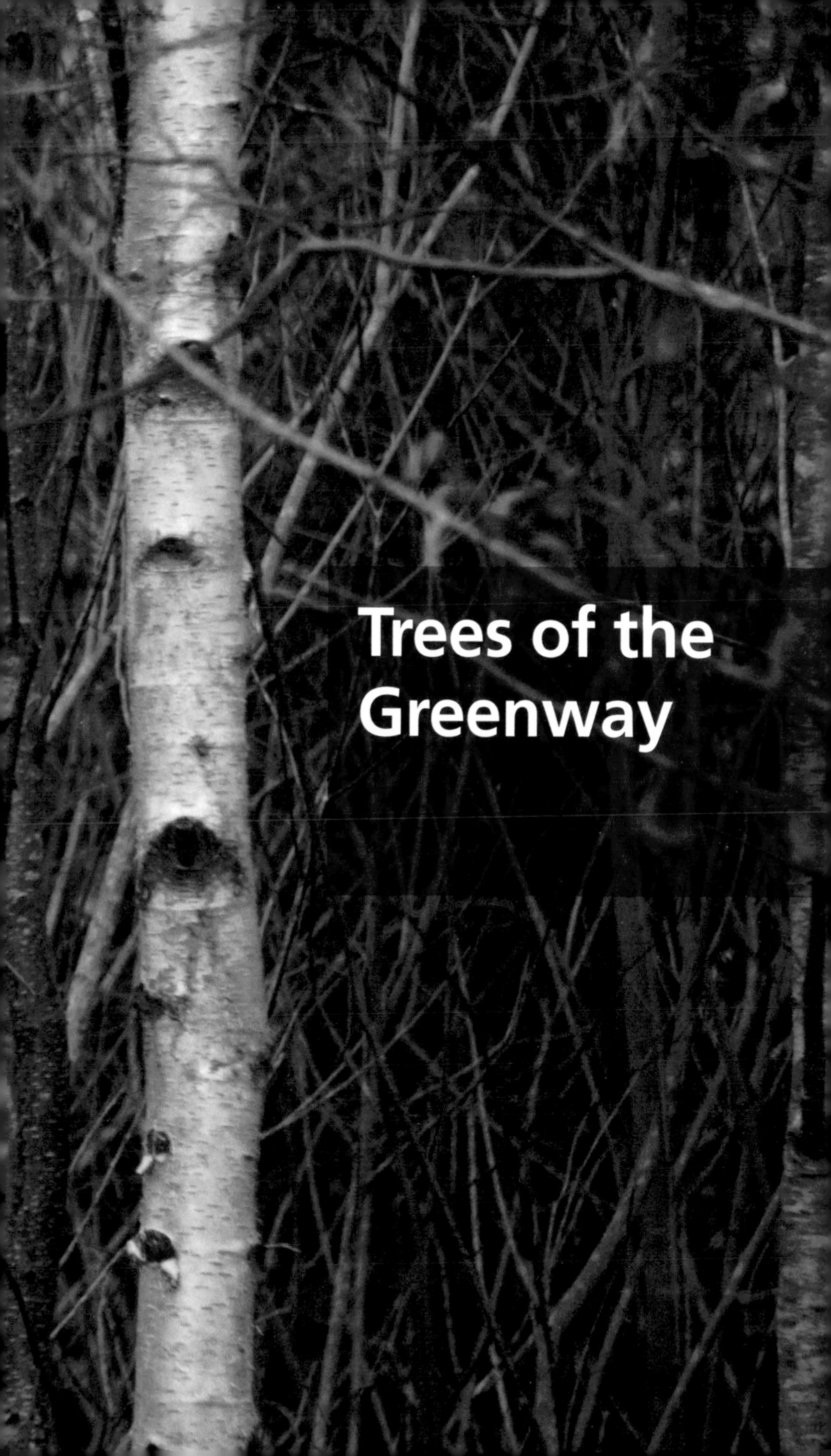
Trees of the
Greenway

After the last great Ice Age, Ireland became densely forested with mixed broadleaf trees and Scots Pine. It was said that a squirrel could scurry from one side of the country to the other without once coming to ground!

Trees were an important aspect of early Irish life, providing shelter, fuel, food, clothing, weapons, furniture and medicine. They were regarded with such reverence that the letters of the first Irish alphabet, developed between 100 and 300 A.D., were named after trees. This ancient alphabet was called Ogham and consisted of a series of short horizontal or slanting lines cross-hatching or stemming from a long central line, much like a tree itself.

In ancient Irish law, trees and various shrubs and vines were accorded certain values according to their economic worth, and a system of laws governing their use and penalties regarding their damage was enforced.

How profoundly that world has changed, there being neither trees nor squirrels in abundance any more. By 1900 only about 1% of tree cover remained in the country. This was due to a number of factors such as a huge increase in human population, leading to the clearing of woodland for farming.

This influx in population was partly due to the advent of England's growing prosperity and expansion of power, which resulted in colonists invading Ireland and displacing native land-holders.

Engaged in a race with Spain, Portugal and France to colonise newly-discovered lands, England needed forests to provide wood for ship-building as well as barrel-making for the preservation of food on long voyages. They also needed wood to make charcoal for smelting iron ore to produce weapons and other hardware.

The new settlers chopped down the forests and exported the timber to England, where huge profits were to be made. In addition, England needed more land to produce more food, and thus by the middle of the 18th century, Ireland's deforestation was well under way. Today it is one of the least forested countries in Europe.

Most of the trees along the Greenway are native species, whilst others, such as Sycamore and Beech, have been introduced from other parts of Europe and have become naturalised. I have included a selection of trees which can be spotted along the Greenway and provided their common, scientific and Irish names. Where applicable I have also noted the Ogham letter derived from the tree, along with the Irish name of the letter.

Alder, Common

Alnus flutinosa
Fearn
(F - Fern)

Alder trees love to be by fresh water. Because of this and their vigorous growth, they are a good tree to help drain a water-logged field, and they further improve the soil with their ability to fix atmospheric nitrogen. A member of the Birch Family (Betulaceae), they are a small, spreading tree with smooth, rounded, toothed leaves. Male trees have long, yellowish catkins, while female trees have purplish oval catkins. Both appear before the leaves, from February to March.

The wood has been used for making shields, bowls and charcoal, while the bark and catkins produce a black dye. They were also used in coppicing for firewood and small poles and make a good shelter-belt.

Ash, Common

Fraxinus excelsior
Fuinseog
(O – Onn)

The Ash, surprisingly enough, is a member of the Olive Family (Oleaceae). It is a large tree, growing up to 40m (130ft) and can live to be over 400 years old. Its leaves are opposite and slightly toothed, with 6–12 pairs and one at the tip. The

Ash

bark is smooth and grey, becoming fissured with age, and the branches are recognisable in winter by their prominent paired black buds. The tufted purplish petal-less flowers, which can be male, female or hermaphrodite, appear before the leaves from April to May; it is one of the last trees to develop leaves in the spring and one of the first to shed them in autumn. Its fruits are a one-winged key, a favourite winter food of Bullfinches.

Ash's strength and resilience makes it an ideal wood for the manufacture of tool handles and hurleys, and it has also been used to craft spears, coach-axles, furniture and oars.

Beech

Fagus sylvatica
Fháibhile

Although Beech is not native to Ireland, it was widely planted in the 18th century, having come from the south of England. It may have come over even earlier, with the Norman invasion in the 12th century. However, it has become naturalised and can crowd out native species, due to its massive growth (up to 40m/130ft) and spreading crown.

It is a member of the Beech Family (Fagaceae), which includes Oaks. Its bark is smooth and light grey. Male flowers and female flowers are pale green and grow in separate clusters on the same tree. In April and May they open up with the leaves, which are oval, deeply veined and lightly toothed with a pointed tip. The small fruit is a triangular shiny brown nut encased in a bristly brown husk which splits into four 'petals'.

While the wood is not suitable for outdoor use, it is popular for wood-turning in the form of furniture, bowls, tool handles and spoons. It is also used for veneers. The nuts are edible and fed to livestock. Beeches often retain their dried leaves in winter.

Birch, Silver

Betula pendula
Beith Gheal
(B – Beith)

A graceful, slender tree with slightly drooping branches, this is a member of the Birch Family (Betulaceae).

The pendulous yellow male catkins and erect green female catkins appear in early spring, before the leaves, which are bright green and spade-shaped, with uneven teeth.

The small seeds, which mature in the autumn, are an important food source for birds such as Finches, Redpolls and Siskins. The bark is shiny purplish-black when young, becoming papery and white when older, with black diamond-shaped marks. It is tolerant of harsh conditions and is one of the first trees to colonise disturbed ground, providing shelter for other trees, which may replace them over time.

It is closely related to the Downy Birch (*Betula pubescens*), which tends to favour damper soils and can be distinguished from Silver Birch by its erect growth and downy branches.

Silver Birch was associated with birth, purity and youthfulness. Its very strong wood was used for many objects, such as flooring, furniture, doors, clogs, musical instruments and tool handles. Its twigs were bound together to make brooms, while tannin from the bark was used for preserving leather and fishing lines.

It had many uses in traditional medicine, and a substance in its bark called betulinic acid is being studied as a possible treatment for several forms of cancer.

Top image © Jonathan Billinger, CC BY-SA 2.0

Blackthorn

Prunus spinosa
Draighean
(Str – Straif 'sulphur')

Blackthorn, a member of the Rose Family (Rosaceae), is a small tree, growing to about 4m (13ft). Its bark is dark black, and its branches are spiky with thorns.

It sends shoots out from its base or root, which grow new stems that form dense thickets. These provide safe nesting for birds such as Finches, Song Thrushes and Blackbirds, as well as runs for other wild animals.

The delicate white flowers appear in early spring before the small finely-toothed oval dull-green leaves. They are followed in the autumn by sour purple-black fruits called sloes, which resemble small plums. Blackthorn thrives in almost any habitat except for wet or chalky soils.

Traditionally it has been associated with the fairies and, along with the Hawthorn, is said to bring bad luck to anyone who would be so unwise as to cut one down. Because its wood is light-weight but very hard, it was used to make shillelaghs, a cross between a walking stick and a club. The fruits are still used to make sloe jam, sloe gin and sloe wine.

Elder

Sambucus nigra
Trom
(R – Ruis 'redness')

A member of the Honeysuckle Family (Caprifoliaceae), Elder is a small tree, from 3m (10ft) to 10m (33ft) in height. It grows on waste grounds and in hedges, scrub and woods.

Its bark is greyish-brown, with deep cracks and cork-like ridges. The long, pointed serrated leaves are opposite each other along a stem in 2 to 3 pairs with one at the tip. The creamy-white saucer-shaped flower-heads appear from May to July and have a strong scent, which attracts insects to graze on their nectar. These give way in late summer to clusters of purple-black berries, much loved by birds.

Elder trees were traditionally regarded as malevolent and unlucky, although they were commonly planted around houses to keep witches away.

Although its wood was not considered of much use, the tree's chief value resided in its medicinal and nutritional properties. Its flowers were used to make wine, cordial and fritters, whilst the berries were made into jam and wine.

Extracts from the flowers, berries, leaves, bark and roots were widely used to treat a variety of ailments, including skin conditions, flu, bronchitis, rheumatism and gout.

Hawthorn

Crataegus monogyna
Sceach Gheal
(H – hÚath 'fear')

Also known as Whitethorn or Maybush, this is another tree of the Rose Family (Rosaceae). It is a short, spiny tree, from 2–10m (6.5–33ft) tall.

It is commonly found in hedgerows, scrub and on the edges of woods. It can be gnarled and bent almost horizontal with the wind, though given space and shelter it has a spreading, rounded crown.

Its leaves are small, glossy green on top, with 3 to 7 deep lobes and toothed edges. The veins on the bottom of the leaves have tufts of hairs. Clusters of fragrant white flowers appear in May, well after the leaves are out. This is an easy way to distinguish them from Blackthorns, which blossom before the leaves are out. The flowers are followed by bright crimson berries, called haws, much favoured by birds.

The wood is quite tough and was used for tool handles, mill-wheel teeth, carvings, cabinet work and the ribs of small boats, whilst boxes were made from the roots. It makes good firewood and charcoal, though its chief use was for hedging. A jelly was made from its haws.

Like the Blackthorn, it is strongly connected with the fairies, and it was and still is considered extremely unlucky to cut a Hawthorn tree. Because of this they are very often worked around and left alone. It is common to find a lone Hawthorn in a field, especially at archaeological sites.

Hazel

Corylus avellana
Coll
(C – Coll)

A member of the Hazel Family (Corylaceae), this is a small tree, usually only reaching 6m (20ft). It often grows as an understory in woodland but can also be found in scrub and hedgerows.

It especially likes limey soils and grows abundantly in the Burren in Co. Clare. The bark is reddish- or greyish-brown, smooth and shiny, and peels off as the tree ages. The leaves are broad, saw-toothed and rounded, with downy hairs.

Male and female catkins grow on the same tree, though they must be pollinated by other hazel trees. The brownish male catkins form in the autumn and as early as January or February begin to elongate and turn pale yellow. The female catkins are small buds with bursts of bright red stigmas. These develop into nuts partially encased in a frilly husk, green at first and turning brown in the autumn.

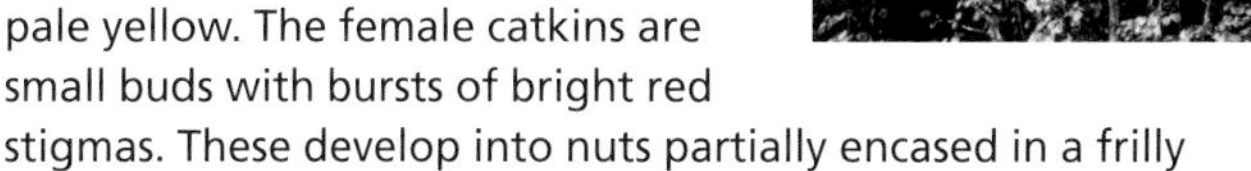

Hazelnuts have been an important source of human food since earliest times and also provide nourishment for Red Squirrels and other small rodents.

Hazel can be coppiced, and its rods were used in the construction of wattle and daub houses. They were also used for other types of wickerwork and basket-making, as well as for Eel and Lobster traps. It was a highly valued tree for all its different uses.

Holly

Ilex aquafolium
Cuileann
(T – Tinne 'iron bar')

Holly is one of our few evergreen native trees. The only member of the Holly Family (Aquafoliaceae), it can grow up to 15m (49ft) and can live for more than 300 years.

It is a hardy tree, often growing beneath other tall trees, in hedges, scrub or exposed places where few other trees can survive. As it can reproduce by growing shoots from its root system, multiple smaller stems often grow up, forming a thicket surrounding the original trunk.

The lower leaves are oval, spiny and leathery, a glossy deep green on top and a lighter, matt green underneath. Higher leaves have wavy, smooth edges. The sharp evergreen leaves provide a safe shelter for birds.

The male and female trees both bear tight clusters of tiny white or pinkish sweetly-scented flowers from May to August, which are highly attractive to bees. However, only the female trees develop berries, which ripen from green to bright red in the autumn and remain on the tree through the winter. They are poisonous to humans, but not to birds, and are especially liked by the Mistle-thrush.

With its fresh green leaves and bright red berries, Holly has long been associated with the winter solstice, and later with Christmas, when it was brought indoors as a symbol of rejuvenation and new growth to come.

The leaves were used as fodder for livestock. Its hard, fine-grained pale wood was prized for carving and was also used to fashion darts and spears.

Oak

Quercus petraea – Sessile Oak
Dair Ghaelach
Quercus robur – Pedunculate Oak
Dair Ghallda
(D – Dair)

Top: Sessile Oak, © Willow, CC BY-SA 3.0. Bottom: Pedunculate Oak, © Trish Steel, CC BY-SA 2.0

The Sessile Oak is so named because its acorns grow not on stalks (peduncles) but directly on the outer twigs (thus, sessile). The acorns of the Pedunculate, or Common Oak, however, are borne on long stalks.

The leaves of the two trees also differ in that the leaf of the Sessile Oak tapers to an unlobed base on a long stalk, while those of the Pedunculate Oak have pronounced lobes at their base and almost no stalk. Both have oblong, lobed leathery leaves, dark green on top and paler underneath.

They both bear male and female catkins from May to June. Both species grow to a great height – the Sessile to 40m (131ft) and the Pedunculate to 45m (147.6ft).

The Sessile Oak can reach an age of over 1,000 years and is more commonplace in Ireland today, especially along the west coast. The Pedunculate Oak is found mainly in the midlands. They are both of the Beech Family (Fagaceae). Oaks support a greater variety of wildlife than any other Irish tree.

Because of the many uses of Oak wood, it was accorded a place of honour in the Brehon laws. Its timber was valued for building houses and boats, for firewood, for charcoal in smelting, and for making barrels and furniture, while the bark was widely used for tanning leather and for producing a black dye. The Sessile Oak is Ireland's national tree.

Rowan/Mountain Ash

Sorbus aucuparia
Caorthann
(L – Luis -- related to luise, 'blaze')

The Rowan is yet another member of the Rose (Rosaceae) family. It is distinguished by its creamy-white flower-heads in spring, followed by bright red berries and flaming foliage in the autumn.

It grows in woodland, on moors and rocky mountainsides, seemingly straight out of the rock in some places. It bears a superficial resemblance to Ash – hence its alternative name Mountain Ash – in that its leaves are pinnate.

Individual leaflets are elongated and serrated and grow in 5–7 pairs along a stem with one terminal leaflet. Its bark is silvery, smooth and shiny. It can grow up to 15–20m (49–65.6ft) but is often much smaller, especially in exposed places.

Traditionally red was deemed to be the best colour to ward off evil, so the Rowan, with its bright crimson berries, was considered to have strong protective powers and was planted near houses to protect the occupants from the spirits of the dead.

The berries are a favourite food of birds, especially the Mistle Thrush, Blackbird, Chaffinch and Siskin. The berries are rich in vitamin C and were used to make jelly and a type of fermented drink similar to perry.

Rowan wood is strong and resilient and was used in turning and carving and to fashion tool handles, cart-wheels, bowls, platters and walking sticks. Its branches were used for water-divining.

Scots Pine

Pinus sylvestris
Giúis
(A – Ailm 'pine')

Of the Pine Family (Pinaceae), this is Ireland's only native pine. An evergreen, it grows up to 40m (131ft) tall, with a conical shape at first and later rounding or flattening out, with branches high up and spaced well apart from each other.

The bark is reddish and resinous. Its blue-green sharp-tipped needles are long and grow in pairs. It bears cones with glossy scales, each with an upturned prickle. These remain on the tree for several years before opening.

Scots Pine can grow on poor soil, on moors, heaths and in forests, and it can reach an age of over 500 years. The stumps of Scots Pine are commonly found in peat bogs, where they grew in abundance up to 7,000 years ago before the bog formed.

It has symbiotic relations with many species of fungus, whereby the fungi, which cannot make direct use of the sun's energy, receive nutrients produced by the tree's photosynthesis, and the tree in turn benefits by receiving nutrients from the soil that it cannot access other than through the fungi.

Because of its high resin content, its wood burns with a strong, clear light. Bog Pine was often dug up and used as torches.

Traditionally, resin was collected from the tree and made into pitch used to caulk boats and preserve wood. Also, turpentine is produced from the resin.

The timber is one of the strongest softwoods and is used in joinery and construction.

Sycamore

Acer pseudoplatanus
Seiceamóir

Sycamore is not a native tree to Ireland, though it has become naturalised, and can be invasive. A member of the Maple Family (Aceraceae), it comes from central and southern Europe, but it is not known just how or when it was introduced here.

It is found in hedgerows and woodland. A spreading fast-growing tree, it reaches up to 35m (115ft) in height, but only lives to about 150 years. Its leaves have a distinctive hand-shaped coarsely-toothed leaf.

The flowers, which can switch sexes, are drooping frothy clusters of lime-green and appear in May. These are followed by winged fruits in pairs, which twirl to the ground like helicopters, where they sprout freely when not consumed by Wood Mice.

The bark is smooth and grey, becoming flakey and pinkish-brown when older.

Its creamy-white wood is hard and strong and highly valued for flooring in dance halls. It was also used for furniture, turning, musical instruments and carving. It is tolerant of salt air and was commonly planted as a shelter-belt.

Willow

Willow Family (*Salicaceae*)
Saileach
(S – Sail)

Top: Grey Willow, . Bottom: Eared Willow

There are a great many varieties of Willow in Ireland, but among the most common are Goat Willow, also called 'Pussy Willow' (*Salix caprea*), Grey Willow (*Salix cinerea*) and Eared Willow (*Salix aurita*). These are also known as Sallow Willows or Sallies.

All prefer damp soil and can be found in ditches, scrub, damp woodlands and hedges. All three are small trees or shrubs, from 2m (6.5ft – Eared Willow) to 10m (33ft – Goat Willow) in height.

Goat Willow has oval leaves with a soft grey down on the underside, and the leaves are broader than on most Willows. The leaves of Grey Willow are long and thin with rust-coloured hairs beneath. The Eared Willow's leaves are rounder, slightly hairy on the underside and have pronounced wrinkles. In addition, they have tiny mouse-ear-shaped leaflets which grow either side of the leaf stem near the base of the leaf. All three have fluffy catkins, which appear before the leaves. Male and female catkins grow on separate trees.

Willow has soft, flexible stems which were widely used for weaving baskets, mats and fences. Willows can be coppiced, and some species of Willows are used to produce biomass, a source of renewable energy.

Salicin, an anti-inflammatory related to salicylic acid in aspirin, has been extracted from the bark of Goat Willow.

All Willows are rich in insect life, which provides many birds with food, notably the Willow Warbler.

Bicycle Hire

Westport

Mr Sean Sammon
James Street
Telephone: 098 25471
Sean also repairs bikes and has a small shop for bicycle parts.

Clew Bay Bike Hire, Ltd.
Distillery Road
Telephone: 098 37675/ 098 24818
Email: info@clewbayoutdoors.ie
Web: www.clewbayoutdoors.com
They also have outlets at Newport and Mulranny, with a drop-off point in Achill. They operate a shuttle service which drops you off with your bicycle so you can cycle back or will collect you after biking in one direction.

The Westport Bike Shop
The Paddock, Newport Road
Telephone: 098 24966
Email: thewestportbikeshop@gmail.com
They hire, sell and repair bikes.

Electric Escapes
Telephone: 098 56611
Email: info@electricescapes.ie
Web: www.electricescapes.ie
Paul Harmon organises electric bike hire and sales, as well as tours.

Westport Bikes 4 Hire

Carrabawn
Telephone: 086 088 0882
Email: info@westportbikes4hire.com
Web: www.westportbikes4hire.com
They will organise drop-off and collection for you.

For bicycle repairs and sales you can also go to J.P. Breheny & Sons, alternatively called Breheny Cycles, on the Castlebar Road. They do not, however, hire bicycles. Their phone number is 098 25020.

Newport

Newport Cycle Hire & Repairs

Castlebar Road (on the corner with Main Street)
Telephone: 086 329 5277
They will collect you if you pre-book.

Greenway Bicycle Hire

Main Street
Telephone: 086 038 2594 or 086 038 2593
Email: greenwaybicyclehire@gmail.com
Web: www.greenwaybicyclehire.com
They will drop off and collect you if you just want to cycle in one direction.

Clew Bay Bike Hire, Ltd.

George's Street
Telephone: 098 37675 or 098 24818
Email: info@clewbayoutdoors.ie
Web: www.clewbayoutdoors.com
They also have outlets at Westport and Mulranny, with a drop-off point in Achill. They operate a shuttle service for drop-off and collection.

Mulranny

Clew Bay Bike Hire, Ltd.

Behind Mulranny Park Hotel
Telephone: 098 37675/ 098 24818
Email: info@clewbayoutdoors.ie
Web: www.clewbayoutdoors.com

Greenway Bike Hire

At Costcutter Supermarket, Mulranny
Telephone: 087 280 7360

Achill

Achill Bikes

Dooagh, Achill Island
Telephone: 098 43301 or 087 243 7686 or 086 172 3087
Email: info@achillbikes.com
Web: www.achillbikes.com
They have a B&B and a mini-bus for drop-off and collection.

Clew Bay Bike Hire, Ltd.

Óstán Oileán Acla (Achill Island Hotel)
Telephone: 098 37675/ 098 24818
Email: info@clewbayoutdoors.ie
Web: www.clewbayoutdoors.com
The hotel is a drop-off point for bicycles. They do not hire them out from there.

Special Thanks

Bill Galloway: For editing and thorough proofreading, being a wonderful walking companion and for endless help and support. Also for some of the photographs in the book.
Fergus Kelly: For superb style and long hours devoted to polishing the design of this book. Also for some very fine photographs.
Dr Derek McLoughlin: For wildlife expertise, proofreading and unflagging support.
Sue Callaghan: For wildlife expertise and encouraging support. Also for allowing me to use her photograph of Irish/Mediterranean Heath.
Jackie Ryan: For being a delightful walking companion on many a long hike.
Joe McDermott: For invaluable historic expertise and advice.
Sean Carolan: For unstinting helpfulness, wildlife expertise, local knowledge and resources, and information about the Old Irish Goat.
John Joyce: For permission to use his magnificent photograph of an Old Irish Goat.
Anna Connor: For being endlessly helpful regarding many aspects of the Greenway and for supplying information, maps and support.
Padraig Philbin: For giving me printouts of maps and spending time going over them with me, discussing Greenway plans.
Dominick O'Grady: For local knowledge and fascinating stories.
Cllr Michael Holmes: For superb local knowledge and stories.
Tommy Hughes: For extensive local knowledge and stories.
Danny Callaghan: For local knowledge and key historic information.

Kathleen McNea: For kindly taking the time to show me her basket-weaving workshop.
Seosamh Ó Dálaigh: For graciously taking time to talk to me about his art gallery.
The Newport Tourist Office: For being so helpful in my research, showing me around the premises and lending me materials.
Pip Murphy: For helpful local knowledge and information.
Lee McDaid: For enthusiastic support and wildlife expertise along the Mulranny to Achill section of the Greenway.
Tadhg Ó Corcora: For information about Lough Gall Bog and bog conservation.
Denis Strong: For information about Lough Gall Bog.
Robert Searns: For allowing me to use his quote at the end of the Mulranny to Achill section and for his enthusiastic support and advice.
Pat Staunton: For information about gates along the new section of the Greenway near Newport.
Deirdre Cunningham: For approving a grant for my Heritage Week exhibition of this book.
Ken Stevenson: For graciously allowing me a glimpse of the Newport tunnel.
Westport Railway Station: For opening the doors of their enchanting little museum to me and for allowing me to use the old photograph of the train at the station.

Special thanks to **Amanda Ryan** and all at the Heritage Council for their generous support of this project.

And to **all the landowners** who have given permission for the Greenway to cross their lands, and to all who have been involved in the project, a huge thank you for making it all possible.

Credits

Photographs and Illustrations

All photographs and images © Iris Galloway, unless otherwise noted.

p44 Starling, © Philip Heron, available at http://commons.wikimedia.org/wiki/File:Colourful_starling.jpeg, licensed under the Creative Commons Attribution-Share Alike 3.0 Unported license.

p45 Common Blue Butterfly, © Ernst Vikne, available at http://commons.wikimedia.org/wiki/File:Common_Blue_(Polyommatus_icarus).jpg, licensed under the Creative Commons Attribution-Share Alike 2.0 Generic license.

p46 'Sybil' the Stoat, © Peter Trimming, available at http://www.geograph.org.uk/reuse.php?id=2988524, licensed under the Creative Commons Attribution-Share Alike 2.0 Generic license.

p47 Long-eared Bat, by Ernst Haeckel, available at http://commons.wikimedia.org/wiki/File:Haeckel_Chiroptera_Plecotus_auritus_1.jpg, public domain.

p58 Small Copper Butterfly, © Evelyn Simak, available at http://commons.wikimedia.org/wiki/File:Small_Copper_Butterfly_(Lycaena_phlaeas)_on_ragwort_-_geograph.org.uk_-_1400695.jpg, licensed under the Creative Commons Attribution-Share Alike 2.0 Generic license.

p59 Lapwing, © Hans Hillewaert, available at http://commons.wikimedia.org/wiki/File:Vanellus_vanellus_(profile).jpg, licensed under the Creative Commons Attribution-Share Alike 3.0 Unported license.

p69 Harry Clarke stained-glass windows in Newport Church, © Fergus Kelly, by kind permission of the photographer.

p88 Viviparous Lizard, © Anaiptol, available at http://commons.wikimedia.org/wiki/File:Driezhas.jpg, licensed under the Creative Commons Attribution 3.0 Unported license.

p95 Rockfleet Castle, © Fergus Kelly

p123 Old Irish Goat, © John Joyce, by kind permission of the photographer.

p124 Irish Heath, © Sue Callaghan, by kind permission of the photographer.

p126 Peregrine Falcon (Falco Peregrinus), © Anne Burgess, available at http://www.geograph.org.uk/reuse.php?id=1946888, licensed under the Creative Commons Attribution-Share Alike 2.0 Generic license.

p127 Golden Plover, © Ferran Pestaña, available at http://commons.wikimedia.org/wiki/File:Chorlitejos_dorados_en_vuelo_-_Eurasian_golden_plover_-_Pluvialis_apricaria.jpg, licensed under the Creative Commons Attribution-Share Alike 2.0 Generic license.

p133 Merlin, © U.S. Fish & Wildlife Service - Pacific Region's, available at http://commons.wikimedia.org/wiki/File:Falco_columbarius_Bandon_Marsh_NWR.jpg, licensed under the Creative Commons Attribution 2.0 Generic license.

p133 Raven, © Atli Harðarson, available at http://commons.wikimedia.org/wiki/File:Krummi_1.jpg, licensed under the Creative Commons Attribution 2.0 Generic license.

p164 Lords & Ladies at Thirlestane, © M.J. Richardson, available at http://www.geograph.org.uk/photo/1873625, licensed under the Creative Commons Attribution 2.0 Generic license.

p164 Arum maculatum, © Paul Henderson, available at http://commons.wikimedia.org/wiki/File:Arummaculatum_1.jpg, licensed under the Creative Commons Attribution-Share Alike 3.0 Unported license.

p170 St John's Wort, © H. Zell, available at http://commons.wikimedia.org/wiki/File:Hypericum_perforatum_003.jpg, licensed under the Creative Commons Attribution-Share Alike 3.0 Unported license.

p186 Blackthorn in bloom, © Jonathan Billinger, available at http://www.geograph.org.uk/reuse.php?id=398463, licensed under the Creative Commons Attribution 2.0 Generic license.

p191 Sessile Oak, © Willow, available at http://commons.wikimedia.org/wiki/File:Quercus_petraea_05.jpg, licensed under the Creative Commons Attribution-Share Alike 3.0 Unported license.

p191 Pedunculate Oak, © Trish Steel, available at http://commons.wikimedia.org/wiki/File:Acorns,_Holt_Heath_-_geograph.org.uk_-_1472667.jpg, licensed under the Creative Commons Attribution-Share Alike 2.0 Generic license.

p195 Grey Willow, © Jolán Dénes, available at http://commons.wikimedia.org/wiki/File:Malpighiales_-_Salix_cinerea_5_-_2011.06.05.jpg, licensed under the Creative Commons Attribution-Share Alike 2.5 Generic license.

References

Beaumont, Jonathan (2002). *Rails to Achill*. Oakwood Press, Monmouthshire, U.K.

Blamey, Marjorie; Fitter, Alastair; Fitter, Richard (1996). *Collins Pocket Guide: Wildflowers of Britain and Northern Europe*. Harper Collins Publishers, London.

Boland, H. & Crowe, O. (2007). *Irish Wetland Bird Survey: Results of waterbird monitoring in Ireland in 2005/06*. Irish Birds 8, pp. 167-178, Ireland.

Browne, Juanita (2005). *Ireland's Mammals. Browne Books*, Calverstown, Kilcullen, Co. Kildare.

"Burrishoole Loop Walks" Brochure, No. 2. Newport Tourist Office, Newport, Co. Mayo.

Cabot, David (1999). *Ireland: A Natural History*. Harper Collins Publishers, London.

Cabot, David (2004). *Irish Birds*. Harper Collins Publishers, London.

Chinery, Michael (General Editor) (1987). *Kingfisher Field Guide to the Plant Life of Britain & Europe*. Kingfisher Books, London.

Conroy, Don & Wilson, Chris (1997). *Wildfile*. Mentor Press, Dublin.

Culpepper, Nicholas (1653). (1995 edition). *Culpepper's Complete Herbal*. Wordsworth Reference, Hertfordshire.

Dempsey, Eric & O'Clery, Michael (2007). *Finding Birds in Ireland*. Gill and Macmillan, Dublin.

Foss, Peter J. & Doyle, Gerard J. (1990). "The history of *Erica erigena* R. Ross, an Irish plant with a disjunct European distribution", Journal of Quaternary Science, Volume 5, Issue 1, pp. 1-16.

Fossit, Julie A. (2000). *A Guide to Habitats in Ireland*. The Heritage Council, Ireland.

Galloway, Iris & Kennan, Rob (2009). *Walk the Line: Pocket Guide to The Old Railway Line Walk, Westport*. Westport Civic Trust Ltd., Westport, Co. Mayo.

Gooders, John & Harris, Alan (1986). *Kingfisher Field Guide to the Birds of Britain and Ireland*. Kingfisher Publications, London.

Grieve, Mrs. M. (1937). (1994 edition). *A Modern Herbal*. Tiger Books International, London.

Lucey, John & Doris, Yvonne (2001). "Biodiversity in Ireland." Environmental Protection Agency, Johnstown Castle Estate, Co. Wexford.

Mac Coitir, Niall (2008). *Irish Wild Plants*. The Collins Press, Cork.

Mac Coitir, Niall (2008). *Irish Trees: Myths, Legends & Folklore*. The Collins Press, Cork.

McDermott, Joe & Chapman, Robert (1992). *A West of Ireland Walk Guide: County Mayo – The Bangor Trail*. Comhairle Chontae Mhaigh Eo, Castlebar.

McDonald, Theresa (1997). *Achill: 5000 B.C. to 1900 A.D.* I. A. S. Publications, Ireland.

Mayo County Council. *Draft County Mayo Biodiversity Action Plan*. http://www.mayococo.ie/en/media/Media,12650,en.pdf

Masterson, Fintan (2011). "The History and Architecture of Rosturk Castle, Rosturk, County Mayo (Part 1)", *Cathair na Mart – Journal of the Westport Historical Society*, Vol. 29, pp. 54-70.

Masterson, Fintan (2012). "History of Rosturk Castle, Rosturk, County Mayo (Part 2)", *Cathair na Mart – Journal of the Westport Historical Society*, Vol. 30, pp. 70-78.

Maxwell, W. H, (circa 1832). *Wild Sports of the West*. Frederick A. Stokes Company, New York.

Mayo County Council (2010). *Environmental Report: Draft Renewable Energy Strategy for County Mayo*. http://www.mayococo.ie/res/SEA%20Environmental%20Report%20for%20Renewable%20Energy%20Strategy.pdf.

Mayo News (15 February, 2011). "NATURE Mulranny – Last Stronghold of the Old Irish Goat?" http://www.mayonews.ie.

Nairn, Richard (2005). *Ireland's Coastline: Exploring its Nature and Heritage*. The Collins Press, Cork.

Natura Environmental Consultants (2005). "Habitat Survey Guidelines." The Heritage Council, Ireland.

Ó Conghaile, Pól (15 October, 2011). "Secret Ireland: The Great Western Greenway." http://independent.ie.

O'Reilly, Peter (1987). *Trout and Salmon Loughs of Ireland*. Unwin Hyman, London.

Poole, Russell & de Eyto, Elvira. "Case Study Description: The Burrishoole Catchment". Marine Institute, Furnace, Newport, Co. Mayo. http://www.diadfish.org/maj2006_fichiers/maj_11_06_slime/bburrishoole.pdf.

Scallon, Christine (2003). *Herbal Cures: Healing Remedies from Ireland.* Newleaf (Gill and Macmillan), Dublin.

Smith, George F.; O'Donoghue, Paul; O'Hora, Katie; Delaney, Eamonn (2011). "Best Practice Guidance for Habitat Survey and Mapping." The Heritage Council, Ireland.

Sterry, Paul (2004). *Collins Complete Guide to Irish Wildlife.* Collins, London.

Sutton, David (1988). *Field Guide to the Wild Flowers of Britain & Northern Europe.* Parragon, London.

Viney, Michael (2003). *Ireland.* The Blackstaff Press, Belfast.

Viney, Michael (2009). *Wild Mayo.* Mayo County Council, Castlebar.

Viney, Michael (12 February 2011). "A Harsh, Wet Winter Makes it No Country for Old Irish Goats." http://irishtimes.com.

Wilkinson, John & Tweedie, Michael (1994). *Butterflies & Moths of Britain and Europe.* Diamond Books, London.

Williams, Lauren (2009). "NS II Freshwater Pearl Mussel Sub-Basin Management Plans." Lauren Williams, Dingle.

Online References

http://www.absoluteastronomy.com
http://www.achilltourism.com/achillfacts.html
http://www.agriculture.gov.ie
http://aran.library.nuigalway.ie
http://www.askaboutireland.ie
http://www.aughty.org
http://www.batconservationireland.org
http://beheco.oxfordjournals.org
http://www.biodiversityireland.ie
http://www.biology.ie
http://www.birdguides.com
httpl://www.birdwatchireland.ie
http://www.bonaneheritagepark.com
http://botanical.com
http://www.british-trees.com
http://www.butterflyireland.com
http://www.cancer.org
http://www.conserveireland.com
http://www.castlewardenflora.com

http://www.cvni.org
http://www.discoverireland.ie
http://www.epa.ie
http://www.failteireland.ie
http://www.fionasplace.net (Irish Place Names)
http://www.fisheriesireland.ie
http://www.fishinginireland.info
http://www.flora.dempstercountry.org
http://forum.irishmilitaryonline.com
http://www.gardenplansireland.com
http://greenwayteam.com
http://www.heartland.ie
http://hedgerowmobile.com
http://www.herbalremediesinfo.com
http://www.herbsarespecial.com.au
http://www.herbs2000.com
http://www.herbs-treatandtaste.blogspot.com
http://www.ipcc.ie (Irish Peatland Conservation Council)
http://www.irelandswildlife.com
http://www.irishbogrestorationproject.ie
http://www.irishbutterflies.com
http://irishislands.info
http://www.irishoakforests.com
http://www.irishwildflowers.ie
http://www.irishwoods.com
http://www.itmonline.org
http://www.libraryireland.com
http://www.livingtreeeducationalfoundation.org
http://www.magoo.com
http://www.marine.ie (Marine Institute)
http://www.mayococo.ie
http://www.mayolibrary.ie
http://www.mayowalks.ie
http://medicinalherbinfo.org
http://www.moonfern.co.uk
http://mulranny.ie
http://www.nativewoodlandtrust.ie
http://www.natural-healing-guide.com
http://www.naturalmedicinalherbs.net

http://www.niehs.nih.gov
http://www.noticenature.ie
http://npws.ie (National Parks & Wildlife Service)
http://www.oblue.utvinternet.com
http://www.pfaf.org
http://www.pjonline.com/
http://placename.ie (Placenames Database of Ireland)
http://places.galwaylibrary.ie
http://www.ramsar.org
http://www.sciencedirect.com
http://www.seedaholic.com
http://www.southmayo.com
http://www.studentxpress.ie
http://www.teagasc.ie
http://www.thejournal.ie
http://www.theoildrum.com
http://www.treecouncil.ie
http://www.treesforlife.org.uk
http://tourismpurewalking.com
http://www.virtualheb.co.uk
http://www.wesleyjohnston.com
http://www.wicklowmountainsnationalpark.ie
http://www.wildfibres.co.uk
http://www.wildflowersofireland.net
http://www.woodlandleague.org